THE WILD LAND

Jia Pingwa is a formidable cultural figure in China, where he is widely regarded as one of the most important writers of his generation. Born in 1953, his early stories dealt with the countryside around his home city Shangluo in the Shaanxi region. In the 1990s, however, his novels, short stories, poetry and non-fiction became more overtly political, outspoken and challenging to the prevalent climate of censorship, leading to his 1993 novel *The Abandoned Capital* being banned for 17 years by the State Publishing Administration, ostensibly for explicit sexual content.

As his writing became more confrontational, his audience grew exponentially. He also gained critical acclaim from the literary establishment, including winning the Mao Dun Literary Prize, one of the most prestigious writing awards in China, for *Shaanxi Opera* in 2008. Aside from writing, he is a talented professional calligrapher and artist.

This book is part of Shaanxi Stories, a series of translated works by acclaimed authors from the Shaanxi province of China, produced by Valley Press in collaboration with Northwest University, Xi'an. The series editors are Hu Zongfeng and Robin Gilbank. Other books in the series:

MOUNTAIN STORIES, Ye Guangqin
HOW OLD DAN BECAME A TREE, Yang Zhengguang
THE EARTHEN GATE, Jia Pingwa
THE BLOOD RED SUN, Wu Keijing
THE HOWL OF THE WOLF, Hong Ke
IRRATIONAL THINGS, Mu Tao
SUN PALACE, Ye Guangqin
THE HOUR OF THE LOCUST, Yang Zhengguang

The Wild Land

JIA PINGWA

*translated by Hu Zongfeng
and Robin Gilbank*

Valley Press

First published in 2022 by Valley Press
Woodend, The Crescent, Scarborough, YO11 2PW
www.valleypressuk.com

ISBN 978-1-912436-72-9
Cat. no. VP0193

Copyright © Jia Pingwa 2022

The right of Jia Pingwa to be identified as the
author of this work has been asserted in accordance with
the Copyright, Designs and Patents Act 1988.

All rights reserved. No part of this publication may be
reproduced, stored in or introduced into a retrieval system,
or transmitted in any form, by any means (electronic,
mechanical, photocopying, recording or otherwise) without
prior written permission from the rights holders.

A CIP record for this book is available from the British Library.

Cover and text design by Peter Barnfather.
Cover art: *Chinese Garden* (ca. 1780) by Anonymous.
Series edited by Hu Zongfeng and Robin Gilbank.

Printed and bound in Great Britain
by Clays Ltd, Elcograf S.p.A.

Contents

Deformed Buddha 9

Three Years at Northwest University 13

A Little Peach Tree 17

Knocking at the Door 22

On Talking 26

On Friends 29

You Cannot Let Dogs Talk Like People 34

Bald Head 37

On Smoking 41

Walking Into the Future, Alone 43

Asparagus Fern 45

Talking about the Dragon
  in the Year of the Dragon 49

The City of Xi'an 55

Pottery Figures 60

Wall Paintings 69

The Wild Land 74

Shangluo is My Homeland 77

Streams 81

The Fountain 83

My Primary School 87
Stories from Dihua
    I. 96
    II. 98
    III. 99
    IV. 100
    V. 103
    VI. 104
    VII. 105
    VIII. 107
    IX. 108
    X. 110
A Very Ugly Stone 114
Two Generations
    I. 117
    II. 117
    III. 118
    IV. 119
I am not a Good Son 120
Written for My Mother 130

Deformed Buddha

I went to the River Jing to search for characterful stones. Originally, this had been purely for leisure, but when I chanced upon a statue of the Buddha everything took on an air of solemnity. At that moment, I stared up at the sky and spied a cloud, heralding good luck. On the only tree for miles there perched a quiet eagle. Without warning, it launched into flight heading for who knows where.

The hollow Buddha was carved from a grey sedimentary rock and seated on a lotus. The delicate carving of the flower was still tangible; only the edges had been worn away. This indicated that the Buddha was about to wail. But in its decapitated state and with part of its torso missing, it remained silent. I could only discern a left foot, and a right hand resting upon it, from the suggestion of a cross-legged pose.

I heard a boom. It was as a conveyer belt was carrying rocks to stonebreakers that this stone Buddha materialised unannounced. The statuette did not radiate golden light. Instead it was caked in mud and silt, giving it a lugubrious appearance, like a quiet savant who lingers alone in the marketplace and is swallowed up by the crowds. And yet, the shape of the stone was so unique, I felt compelled to rescue it. The Buddha arrived into the world this way.

I dare not describe myself as its rescuer. Did the Buddha even need me to save him? I rinsed the statuette clean and took it home to revere. For a whole day, I lamented how it must have suffered. The next morning, enlightenment touched me. The Buddha had progressed along that conveyer belt on purpose, pausing before the mouth of the breaker to test my responses. It was a relief to find that I was not so slow and obtuse. I believed that benevolence still existed in my character; I had pluck. From then on, I burned incense every day and meditated on both the Buddha and myself.

We could say that the Buddha is perfect, but this specimen was deformed. Could it still be considered a Buddha? A deformed human shell without a body or head is repulsive, yet this deformed Buddha still possessed beauty and grace. As I inspected him, the smoke from the incense drifted slowly upwards. His head and body seemed to have miraculously vanished within the clouds, leaving that dignified and compassionate face suspended in the air. His lowered eyes beamed at me. "Buddha," I said. "The hand of the Buddha is the Buddha himself and so too his foot." When iridescent glass is broken it retains its lustre. Observe, how serenely and peacefully his hand and foot rest there!

We could say that the Buddha is a product of the human mind. This one was only a lump of stone – just a piece of rock of the sedimentary sort and not so hard. Where there is a will there is a way; the instant the carver put his chisel to work he infused the rock with a sense of piety. When it was enshrined in the temple, with the motive of delivering all sentient creatures from torment, the stone was transformed into a Buddha. A banknote is only a piece of paper, and yet it has power in circulation. The territory of a whole village or city, even human life and dignity, can now be purchased.

We could say that since this stone was Buddha-shaped, it must be almighty. But then how could it have rolled and tumbled through the River Jing? Yes, one summer day a flood must have come, laying waste to the Buddha's temple. The statuette, together with bricks, tiles, stone and wooden pillars were plunged into the river, pummelled and sifted into fine sand. Except the stone Buddha survived. The character *jing* in the name of the River Jing ought to carry the same meaning as its homonym *jing*, "to pass through." It was not that the Buddha was incapable of escaping the disaster. Rather, he wanted to pass through the waterway to find out where he should reside. That was how he came into my hands. In the ancient legend of Liu Yi, a gentleman used this very river to float a message to the Dragon King. Now the Buddha himself had passed along it. The Lady Zhen of the River Luo metamorphosed into a god and faded away in a thread of smoke. Deformed as he was, this Buddha came to my attention in person. I should address him as "the Buddha of the River Jing".

I worshipped the one-handed, one-footed Buddha with my whole heart.

Many people heard that I had recovered a stone Buddha from the River Jing. I looked at the Buddha and declared it as an ancient and highly efficacious artefact. The people burned incense and kowtowed before it, praying that the Buddha would bless them with wealth, rank and fertility. They prayed for whatever was lacking from their lives. My neighbour, Mr Wang, even petitioned for good luck before he went to play *mahjong*. Finally, I realised that the reason for the Buddha's missing head and broken body was because the hordes had pleaded them away. All mortal persons exhibit the utmost piety in the throes of their deepest selfishness. Could the Buddha not recognise their greed? The Buddha was sure to be conscious of this. He dealt with their selfishness in his own manner. Facing those grasping acolytes, he had only himself to sacrifice. Such is the way of the world.

Having consecrated the Buddha in my study and burnt

incense to it every day, I baulked at people's brazen behaviour, never daring to make such pitiful wishes of my own. That was until the Buddha intoned in a dream: "No, I am not being treated as a Buddha!"

This morning when I got up and slotted the incense into place, I knelt and clasped my hands. I said, "Buddha, if this is the case, I must make a wish. Since the divine is entitled to own beauty and a sacrificial spirit, let him bless my soul and body so they rest in peace and safety. Bless me as a man of the world to savour all the joys and tribulations of human life."

All men are busy. I am busier than most. As long as the Buddha is close by, I will not become weak and timid. I will not flee, but fulfill my obligations with aplomb.

Three Years at Northwest University

On 28th April 1972, a vehicle carried a nineteen-year-old boy to Northwest University. He, together with his shabby green suitcase, found himself in an unfamiliar place.

So far in life his fate had been precarious. He did not lose his head when presented with this dream-like opportunity. Acute loneliness and melancholy caused him to view the world with apprehension. He counted the number of steps it took to move from classroom to dormitory (524) and from classroom to library (303). As he kept his head perpetually bowed, he discovered thousands of ants scuttling across the campus. All varieties of shoes cut across his line of vision and he would stroll away, reluctant to see the people they belonged to, his walk ungainly. The burden of a gargantuan schoolbag pressed one of his shoulders down, tilting the other skyward.

He only climbed the stage once to participate in the choral competition. Although his mouth opened, no sound was released. Nobody noticed him and inconspicuousness was exactly what he craved. He was a boy from the countryside who had never attended senior high school. This lacuna left him in thrall to everybody else's knowledge. Quietly, he would consign himself to the corner of a reading room and when he had to knock on a teacher's door, he would merely poke at the wood with a single pattering finger. His classmates' rowdy discussions would be listened to in silence. Their mockery and jeers failed to upset or dishearten him. When he scored an unusually poor mark in a politics assignment, he stuck his answer paper above his bed. The object of his shame could look down on him from dawn to dusk.

Another time, he took the post of dormitory prefect. Of course, he discharged his duties with great care, his only regret was not owning a mosquito net. The pests assailed him relentlessly every summer night. Despite being pushed to extreme aggravation, he kept his composure. He wondered: "Is there any way that all these tiny pests can gnaw me into oblivion? Perhaps they have already bitten someone more knowledgeable than me and have become wise. They could be passing a touch of that onto me!" In winter, his quilt was too thin. During the long night, he always felt chilly below the knee and curled up into a foetal position. This surely inhibited his growth, but on the other hand, strengthened his inner kung fu powers.

He had no intention of becoming a writer, but he read any book he could lay his hands on, poring over the pages and jotting down notes. All the while, he remained tight-lipped about what he was doing. Ambling alone in the forest groves of the campus at sunset, he scrutinised all the scars on the bark of the poplars. It was his belief that they were sentient eyes, the eyes of the gods who governed the heavens and the earth. Feeling enriched and determined, he stared up at the sky, perceiving pouncing tigers and leaping dragons in the clouds.

In the early days of his arrival, he was strong and healthy. But as no one was willing to pass the ball to someone so diminutive, his interest in basketball dried up. He couldn't clear the vaulting horse and was shocked to lose ping-pong matches to his female classmates. When it was time to donate blood, he gave 300cc and used the whole fee to purchase books. Soon afterwards, he contracted a serious disease from which he was never to recover. That proved a blessing in disguise. He could now live in a single room, exempt from morning exercises and the 10pm curfew. His creative writing entered its gestation. Nowadays, some critics accuse his articles of having "the air of a sick man". The root cause of this lay in how his career as an author began.

The most unfortunate thing was the constant churning in his stomach. After class, he was forced to queue in a long line to buy food, clanging his chopsticks impatiently against his bowl. He would swiftly polish off a block of cornbread with a ladleful of mixed fried vegetables. He had his own way of giving himself a treat. Whenever a poem or an article of his was published, he would use the forty-five cents royalty to buy one bowl of rice and one of egg soup in a restaurant in Bian Family Village. Thanks to the seductive quality of rice and vegetables, he wrote prodigiously. His poems, however, got no further than the bulletin board in his classroom.

In later years, what he could never forget were all the teachers, young and old. Moreover, he felt an attachment to everyone in his class, whether male or female. In his dreams, he remembered the wooden chair of the reading room on the library's second floor, a grotesque carbuncle of a stone lurking in the forest, the thick trunk and wiry branches of the poplar tree outside his dormitory window, and the shattered carapace of a cicada on its leaves.

Fifteen years have passed since university. In all that time, he felt unable to confess to tearing an article out of the library newspaper. For one whole morning, he plotted how to execute the theft. He also lied about losing a library book, paying fines on it three times when it was still on his shelf.

As a student, he had started to smoke on the sly.

When a girl with long pigtails tantalised his eye in the

distance, he would pen a love poem for her that would surprise even himself.

In September 1975, he graduated. He left the university, still carrying his shabby green case. Once more, he found himself in an unfamiliar place.

A Little Peach Tree

I have often wanted to write a piece about my little peach tree but have never got around to it. This thought fills me with contrition, and I comfort myself by saying: "It is high time I composed something."

It rained today. The patter of raindrops started first thing in the morning. Standing outside, I was glad and murmured: "The spring showers have come so early this year." As the rain dampened my hair, I thought about taking a stroll. But the downpour became heavier and fell torrentially for the whole day. I closed the wooden door and sat down by the window to gaze at my little peach tree. Its branches were being buffeted by the wind and rain, and as the blossoms were shed one by one, most of them became stuck in the muddy puddle below, twirling here and there in the brown water.

The tree appeared far more gaunt than yesterday; its radiance was gone entirely. It was a pity that she was so tiny and only broke into blossom once a year. I sighed and felt helpless; I couldn't bear to watch it anymore. Oh, how haughty I had acted in previous days. Really, I was simply a coward.

One autumn day many years ago, when we were still children, Grandma came back from the market with a peach for each of us. "Eat," she insisted. "It's an enchanted peach. Hold the stone in your mouth when you go to sleep and you will have a dream. If peach blossom appears in your dream, then you will be happy for the rest of your life."

Our moods became serious and we went to bed with the

stones in place. But I could not drop off. I was worried I might not have such a sweet reverie, though I was not ready to abandon all hope. And so, I got up and went outside to bury the peach stone in a corner of the yard, believing that any future dream would be safely stowed away there.

Autumn passed, and another winter too. Every child has their own kind of naïve joy; I was distracted and forgot about the peach stone business. One spring morning, as Grandma was sweeping the yard, she chanced upon a small green shoot in the corner. "What is this?" she cried out.

Suddenly, it all came back to me. A new life was sprouting out of the earth.

The plant grew as though it was the victim of some grievance. Its top was curved over, grasping back at its own stem tightly. The next day it flexed itself, so it seemed slender and yellow. The gentlest of touches would be enough to snap it.

Everyone chuckled. "A peach tree like this is good for nothing," Grandma reflected. "The seed was decent, but it burst out in such a frenzy and won't yield any fruit to speak of. Grafting is what it needs."

However, I refused to accept this and stubbornly maintained that it would flourish in the future. After that, nobody took any notice of it. The peach tree was in an awkward dilemma. My folks were more concerned about pot plants. Grandfather, being fond of flowers, made sure our rooms, courtyards and entrances were lush with blooms and foliage. Each spring when his hobby plants were breaking into bud, many people would come over to savour the sight. Early every morning he would bellow orders for us to move the containers out of the house one by one, and return them again in the evening. My little peach tree never crossed his mind. Quietly, it grew anyway.

During springtime, it certainly wasn't tardy any longer, rocketing up two more feet. I was delighted that it was mine, for this was the offspring of the stone that should have begotten a dream. No doubt, my sisters and brothers who lay down with the pit in their mouth had long forgotten what they dreamt that night. My peach tree stood as an everyday reminder to me of the magical bounty from the market. My prediction spell was living-green and if it broke into blossom, it would confirm my future happiness.

It was at that point that I went away to study in the city. When I came out from the mountains into the metropolis, it dawned on me how miniscule I was; the world beyond the mountains was so vast and the cityscape so full of sights. I began to find the mettle in my soul. I vowed to study hard and to strive vigorously for a stellar career after graduation. Our country courtyard and the little peach tree inside disappeared from my mind.

Eventually, it occurred to me how naïve I was being. The world is a huge tome and I couldn't even muddle my way through the opening line of it. As I aged, my temper worsened, and I often found myself sitting in solitude with overcast and feeble thoughts.

Duly, my grandmother passed away, and misfortunes never come in isolation. My journey home took all night. With little time to spare, she was buried before I arrived. On seeing the shambolic state of the house and imagining Grandma's careworn face, I dissolved into tears in the memorial hall.

At dusk, I rested by the window and on raising my head, I spotted the peach tree. To my astonishment, it was still alive. The crooked trunk was fighting to prop up its branches but it had managed to reach the top of the courtyard wall. How had it survived all these years? Gone were Grandpa's floral displays; plant pots were piled up against the wall. Still it grew. My younger brother told me: "It ought to have blossomed by now, but the pig snapped it with his snout." To their mind, it wasn't rooted in a suitable place, nor was it pleasing to the eye. They wanted to chop it down, but Grandma had protested. She had tended to the tree and kept it watered.

Ah, little peach tree, how could I have forsaken and forgotten about you so casually as I went drifting around a foreign land?

Looking at the peach tree brought thoughts of the grandmother to whom I had been denied a farewell. I felt a deep combined melancholy and remorse for both Grandma and the little peach tree.

Weak as it was and sparse of bud, it nevertheless erupted into blossom overnight.

Once I travelled all the way to the foothills of the Zhongnan Mountains to see an expanse of oleander blossoms. I have enjoyed the nectarines at Mawei Slope. The fruit trees' flowers grew rampant as an inferno, but my poor little straggly peach was the seedling of an enchanted stone. Her blossoms were a weak white colour with papery thin petals. There was no hint of flesh and blush, like a sick girl whose pale face nonetheless wears a bitter smile. I could not help shedding pearly tears at the sight.

It was a relief that the blossom did not fade quickly, as it was the only plant to flower, if forlornly, in the corner of the courtyard. Whenever I looked at it, I never once saw a bee hovering in an expression of affection or a butterfly flapping near. What a poor little peach tree.

Today, I cannot help but shiver. Was this flowering, struggling plant the spirit of the dream I cherished years ago?

Under the heavy rain, the buds are being discarded. I thought these spring torrents would render the colours more vibrant and intensify the bouquet. But who could have predicted its baleful fate? The tree cannot relish the blessings of the shower; it cannot feel this as catharsis. It offers its petals, fragments of itself, up to the wind and the rain. In my heart, I cry for my grandmother.

The rain continues. Hundreds and thousands of times my little peach tree has been bent over and struggled to get up. All the blossoms, now thoroughly saturated, have been cast aside. The tree wears the expression of a swan with its eyes wide open, watching its own feathers being plucked out one by one until completely naked and withered.

I discover that a bud has pulled through on the uppermost branch. With its tender yellow and pink hues, it shivers in the rain, shaking off all the rainwater from its body. Several times, it nearly falls to the earth, but resists. It is like a lighthouse amid the waves, flashing its colourful stripes in a light it seems to emit by itself.

Some consolation is then found. Oh, little peach tree, how should I thank you? You have a single surviving bud. Will you break into flower first thing tomorrow? Will your future blossoms be rich and colourful? Will they be full of scent? My dear, will you become spellbinding? Will you bear fruit? Can I still call you the spirit of my dream?

Knocking at the Door

What do people fear the most? The answer is: the sound of knocking at the door. I have moved five times while living in the city. Each time to a single- or two-bedroom apartment with one sitting room. All day long, my door was pounded like a drum. Every Spring Festival, I would go to the market to buy a pair of "door guardians". Once in place, the heroes Qin Qiong to the right and Jing De to the left were effective at barring spirit visitors, though had no power over humans. Qin Qiong had his armour hammered into pieces by insistent fists. Knockers tended to follow a particular etiquette; the first few taps were always polite and civilised, but when the door refused to budge, the pace became urgent and the sound heavy with impatience. At last, they would deliver a kick to the door.

These days, visitors might ask me for help with one thing or another. But an unwanted guest is about as welcome as a policeman with a search warrant, or a eunuch delivering an imperial edict. How pitiful was the tree whose wood became the beleaguered door of my home. In its previous life, it must have been an abused wife or else a defendant flogged mercilessly in the courtroom.

I used to open the door as soon as the knock sounded. Rushing out from my study, I would shout: "Coming, coming." But the waiting visitors were an odd crowd; characters from every walk of life. They were troublesome to me and yet I was always compelled to keep company. My hair was whitening, one strand at a time. I learnt then never to open up for those without an appointment.

The sound of knocking distracted me from reading and writing. I could only wait for the culprit to leave. Thieves also beat at the door. If there was no answer, they would jemmy their way in. I am not afraid of burglars on the hunt for loose change or a fortune, for I have neither. Thieves rarely set out to rob time, but those with that intention prove themselves very successful. They knocked relentlessly. It was at this point that my extreme irritation would morph into admiration. I thought about timing their persistence and marvelled at the stamina of their hands. Finally, the knocking would cease and I would assume their defeat. After a while, however, it would begin again. Perhaps they were only taking a brief respite or maybe they decided I was asleep somewhere in the house, or in the bathroom; they took a breather before resuming. Silence was my only form of resistance. The more I restrained myself, however, the itchier my throat felt, and I had the compulsion to cough. My bladder would start to tug, but I couldn't risk emptying it. I had this horrid feeling, like I was an escaped convict.

A cunning rabbit keeps three warrens. I try to heed this lesson, my life now no better than a bunny's. In such a sprawling city, with thousands upon thousands of rooms and apartments, how is it that I cannot find a space to sleep, to read and to write in peace? Owning a spacious gated courtyard, complete with a vigilant concierge, is simply a pipe dream. I would gladly make do with a desk in a bedsit. Whenever I squat in the lavatory, I imagine how pleasant it would be to fill in the pit and seal the skylight, renovating it into my own personal garret. My apartments always had one or two bedrooms and a sitting room, without a courtyard at the front or a back door to the rear. I am as easy to root out as a turtle in a jar.

I am not actually the kind of man who can cope without friends. When I'm not reading and writing, I will ask three or four pals to come over and drink, chat about women, play chess or *mahjong*. But it is always the case that the friends who you pine for do not come, while those you would rather avoid, turn up. More than once I have refused to open the door, even to my relatives from back home, leaving them standing out in the cold. They are busy folk and so leave after only a few raps. Such is my regret at missing them that I stamp my foot and punch my chest in frustration. There are many whom I cannot stop arriving: fans seeking calligraphy scrolls to serve as sweeteners for their superiors, people delivering party invitations hoping I will add glamour to their event, and idlers who just want to alleviate their boredom. Such people have cartloads of time to squander. If they find you're not in during the morning, they will try again in the afternoon. If today ends in failure, they will seek you out tomorrow. Maybe in the interim, they will crouch outside or downstairs with the mien of a hunter, waiting for his prey.

During the Ming Dynasty, Chen Jiru wrote: "A deep mountain appears behind a closed door."

Some may say this is happening because you're famous. But I'm not a celebrity. How could a person of that ilk occupy such a tiny apartment? Were I an official, visitors might bring lavish gifts and leave as soon as they had gone through their agenda. As they were departing, they would say: "I won't disturb you further, sir, you're too busy. You need rest." The reality is that those who come, carry only empty hands, and polish off my cigarettes and tea. If I were a movie star or a pop singer, my career would be a rowdy affair. How could I create my art amongst such loud disorder?

Chen Jiru longed to be a hermit. Possibly he, like me, found himself interrupted by others. He once surmised: "Most hermits till for themselves." I am not strong, so this is the first factor preventing me from following the eremitic life. I cannot shoot or fish for I abhor killing. That is the second factor holding me back. I am poor, with no more than two *qing* of land and I certainly lack eight hundred mulberry trees. This is my third shortcoming. I can, indeed, make do with water and simple food, though dare not place myself at the mercy of hunger or hardship. This is my fourth problem.

Just like Mr Chen, the best I can expect is to "have a plain meal and write in a quiet place". I've lived dozens of years on unfussy meals, writing first as a hobby and then to make a living. But what an insurmountable problem it is to find a quiet place and be able to stay there alone. Every few years, since I began to write professionally, I have met with criticism, even a thorough tongue-lashing. The door of my fate has always been knocked at. My soul has never been tranquil. The din from constant knocking has truly unsettled my heart. Youngsters wish for perpetual night under a round moon. As for me, I also wish for never-ending night, and for snow and rain. Then my door would be left undisturbed.

How has this happened? I still want to live. I continue to harbour great ambition, but the world always frustrates with its countless machinations. I'm afraid that my door will be knocked at forever. This is my fate. When I am dead, the words on my epitaph will read: "Here lies a man knocked to death."

On Talking

I seldom talk in public because I've never mastered Standard Chinese. When I find myself amongst a crowd, I listen in silence. I laugh when it's necessary and look annoyed when appropriate. Alternatively, I simply remain calm and collected. My mouth and tongue have relinquished their main functions, so instead I chain smoke and guzzle spicy peppers or vinegar.

More than once, I have tried hard to learn the language. The first time was when I arranged to have gold fillings. Then later, having fallen in love, I made another attempt. On garnering a measure of fame, and with it many invitations, I set myself to the task once more. Alas, whenever it started to gel, my tongue would suddenly jam fast in my mouth. Just like a model trying to catwalk on the street, I made a slightly incongruous spectacle. Even I found the sound of my own voice jarring, so I was afraid to speak out and let others listen. Ultimately thwarted, I let it drop. Later, however, it dawned on me that even Chairman Mao could not speak Standard Chinese, so why should I? I reconsidered using my hometown dialect, but that was even more difficult to understand. And so, it is always the case that during conversations, I end up writing out what I am trying to say in long hand. My train of thought and speech are derailed. The passion for both is lost, so I simply fall silent.

Many years ago, a friend who could speak Standard Chinese accompanied me to Beijing. He was my voice box. My only regret was his stammer. Despite slowing down to a halting pace, his speech impediment was obvious. It always gave people the impression that he was short of breath and might be about to pass out at any moment. One day, someone stopped him on Chang'an Avenue and asked for directions. By coincidence, this person had a stutter too. My companion remained silent. Afterwards, I asked him why he hadn't spoken. He replied: "If I had responded, he might have thought I was mocking him." He just stood there with his mouth firmly closed instead. With this pearl of wisdom from my friend, I was even less willing to speak.

One summer's day, a writer named Mo Yan (the characters of his Chinese name literally mean "don't speak") was heading to Xinjiang. He sent me a telegram, instructing me to meet him at the railway station in Xi'an. At that time, I hadn't yet seen him in person, so I wrote out his name on a board and held it up as I walked about the station. For the whole morning, I remained totally silent. I noticed many people staring, but they were silent too. That day, owing to unforeseen circumstances, Mo Yan could not make it to Xi'an. As the afternoon was drawing near, I was compelled to ask one man whether the Number XX train had arrived yet. This fellow turned the board around in my hands and said: "Now that I'm able to speak to you, I must say that I don't know." Only then did the meaning of those two words on my board – DON'T SPEAK – sink in. How wonderful they were to me; what a pity they had been adopted by another author as his pen name. These days, when I travel, I always carry a holdall that was given to me by the Deaf-Mute School. Whenever I leave the label on the bag exposed, I feel at ease.

Since I cannot speak Standard Chinese, I am naturally reluctant to meet strangers, officials or women. Gradually, my social activities have all but evaporated and I have been rendered almost mute. Even so, I find consolation in cursing others. Cursing folk in the dialect of my hometown is cathartic, though now when I express this, I feel crestfallen. I chide myself for being inarticulate, then try to rally. In many of my articles where I describe the place of my birth, I won't use the phrase "poverty-stricken mountain region". Instead, I write: "My birthplace is similar to Mao's birthplace – Shaoshan." When I admit I cannot speak Mandarin, I say: "Standard Chinese is for ordinary people. I am extraordinary!"

A monk once taught me the secret of achieving great things: "Focus your heart on one matter only and close your mouth like a bottle." My daughter wrote these characters on her bedroom wall as her motto. One character was altered, so it read: "Focus your heart on one matter only and close your mouth like a *ping*." Ping is my pet name. My daughter was promising to keep her mouth as tightly closed as her father's.

I have missed out on the benefits of speaking Standard Chinese, yet I've also avoided so much strife. The world is awash with insinuating written comments and gossip that I've never found myself able to share in. When gossip comes my way, I am silent.

On Friends

A friend is like a piece of iron, a nail, a screw, a safety pin. As long as you wish to, you can be the magnet that draws them out from the dirt of this world. Nowadays, young friends on the street share a code of brotherhood. They delight in calling their pals "iron brothers". When I first heard this form of address, I thought it meant that their friendship was unbreakable like welded iron. But then, I thought again of a magnet being jiggled around; some of its load may fall away, while other pieces remain attached no matter how violently you shake. If you lose your magnetism, everything will drop. Last night, I carried a basin of warm water to the balcony to wash my feet. The moon was hanging in the sky and there was another in my basin. It suddenly struck me that this is the kind of symmetry friends should share.

When I lived in the countryside, I had a lot of friends. Now twenty years have passed and one or two of them still keep in touch with me, but as for the rest – I cannot even remember their names. I often think of a friend of mine who passed away. Despite my small stature, he would happily pass me the basketball during a game. For years, we were each other's shadows. We parted ways because of a bunch of mulberries. We made a deal that each of us would have half of the fruit. When I went to wash my hands, he ate his half and then mine. At that time, people were so poor that not going hungry was the top priority. Now, on greeting each other in the city, we refrain from asking "have you eaten?".

In the struggle for fame and affluence, I made lots of friends, but in the process my friends proved themselves as ephemeral as the seasons. Some have come along, some have gone away, yet there was never a time when people were unwilling to accompany me, occupying the benches to my front, so to speak. I totted up a few rough statistics. There have been friends who helped or hurt me when I was in trouble. There have been friends who offered me a hand when I was down-at-heel. There have been friends who have helped me with sundry everyday things, and, what is more, friends who have chosen to use me and inflict an unceremonious kick. Some friends have crossed me, and others caused great trouble by broadcasting my private business, seasoning it with salt and vinegar. It has been my friends who have both raised me up and left me deflated. Some have severed ties when they thought me spent, and others' behaviour has sickened me to shun them. By contrast, it's more complex to break relations with those whose help actually multiplies my troubles, not to mention those who have lent favours in exchange for endless returns.

Human beings are the dominant species across the surface of this earth, yet only those within a tiny radius form your closest associates. Your circle of friends is your entire world. Your battles for success are wrapped up in the feelings of rancour and admiration towards friends. Several people have observed that I am very capable when it comes to making friends, but they don't know that I spend most of my time with bosom friends alone. Frequently, I've thought of myself as being like a cooked fish laid out on the dining table. Someone pokes it with chopsticks and others dig into it with spoons, leaving behind a bare skeleton. Sometimes I sit alone on the toilet and, enjoying my solitary confinement, think how nice it must be to be in prison. Once I admitted myself into hospital under an alias. All the doctors and nurses I met were hidden behind their surgical masks. I was no longer a name but a number – the digits hanging over my bed. Before the month was out, I could tolerate this no longer and so on the twenty-seventh day I scaled the perimeter wall and called every one of my friends. I recall now another person commenting that my greatest misfortune is my inability to make friends. I cannot entirely agree with this view. A few of my friends have brought me hardship, but the greater part made me proud and delighted.

An old story relates how a sick man needed the doctor. He knew of two doctors on the same street. At the home of one, he saw an apparition of many ghosts. He concluded that this fellow must be highly incompetent; the ghosts his unfortunate past patients. At the home of the second doctor, he saw only two spirits hovering. The man consulted the second doctor but was not cured. A bystander advised him to go back to the first doctor with the crowd of ghosts. He explained how this medic had treated thousands and thousands of patients, of whom perhaps fifty he had lost. The doctor who had treated him attempted to cure two patients, neither of whom pulled through. It occurred to me that maybe I am the doctor accompanied by scores of spirits. My friends appear to fall into two categories, one of which is characterised by resilience under my sincere care.

A few friends offer me everyday assistance. For instance, in purchasing coal and lending a hand to haul it upstairs. Some will chauffeur sick relatives to hospital and one found a kindergarten for my child. It goes without saying that I opened doors for them too. I've written calligraphy for them to soft-soap high ranking officials. I've given them my paintings to aid with bank loan applications. I've attended birthday dinners for my friends' fathers-in-law. Maybe they've helped me a lot; maybe I have helped others more. If we have been sincere and honest with each other, there is no need to keep a tally. We are firm friends all the same.

The other category of friends is those soulmates who find themselves incapable of achieving anything concrete, only able instead to cultivate the slick tongue of a parrot. Still, they are happy to share a pot of tea and converse about literature and art because we admire each other's talent. For a long time, I took my friends very seriously, distracted from my relatives, my parents, wife and children. Nevertheless, I gradually found that how one lives one's life is a personal matter. A caring friend may know every blemish on my body without understanding my heart. Whereas soulmates who understand still find themselves doing things contrary to my will. When happiness comes along, you are the one who savours it most deeply, and when suffering arises, you are the one who is most afflicted.

I persevere in making friends – the more the merrier. You could choose to wander through an empty space, alone and forlorn, but people are people for possessing both soul and body. As such, man cannot live without friends, who help us face the adversities of the outside world; the rabid dog, the thicket, the muddy road.

Picasso was a Spaniard, a man of genius and lifelong renown. He could also boast countless friends. Many seem to have been born for such a role, but he had a high turnover of both women and acquaintances. Yet he left a word of wisdom: "A friend is good when he is gone." When I recall estranged friends or those who I've deliberately cut ties with, my heart chills. But I regain my composure when I recall their good deeds. The chill comes from a contradiction: I took my friends as family members, not realising that when all is said and done, a friend is a friend. Friends are spring blossoms that disappear in winter. A friend may not necessarily be a soulmate. Equally, a soulmate may not necessarily be a friend. A soulmate might not always act as a true man. He may feed from and consume me; he may malign me. That counts for nothing. If an emperor can feed an entire country, how many people should I offer my help to?

This morning, I made a new friend. The fellow complained to me about his wife working in a county suburb. The family had gone without a reunion for more than a decade. He asked me to write several pieces of calligraphy for him to offer as gifts to the head of human resources. I wrote them straightaway. In return, he left me a tin of green tea and a pack of refined cigarettes. When he was gone, I called three or four old friends over to share in my cheer. At this moment, they are hastily pedalling their way over here. I will wait for them. Selfishly, I have already brewed and poured a cup of tea for myself and lit a cigarette. In this moment, I think of the quiet sacrifices of true friends. I shall surely burst into laughter when I greet those noisy and boisterous pals at the door.

You Cannot Let Dogs Talk Like People

Almost every household in Xi'an has a dog, so there's no shortage of breeds around. Every morning and every dusk in the parks, along the street, across neighbourhoods, owners are out exercising their pets. The dogs may keep pace with the walker and the walker may sometimes have to keep pace with the dog. Dogs have become members of the family. They eat well, sleep well, and shower daily. Whenever they fall ill, they see a doctor. Lacking as they do a surname, their given names are nevertheless highly individualistic. Records tell us there are eight million residents of the city. Is this accurate? Nobody has taken a census of canines. The true number must be upwards of ten million.

Society is now classless, yet so many sub-groups have emerged. These include fellow villagers or townspeople, classmates, army comrades. They cast out and weave a vast social web. There are supplementary groupings like those who surf online, those who play the stock market, those who pursue Buddhism, those who scale mountains, and those who keep dogs. One proverb states: "Friends fool around like foxes and dogs." Now, friendships are forged via dogs. When the scheduled playdate comes around, dog-made friends assemble in the square with their pets. The animals jump around and bark, hounds and bitches copulate, bowels are discharged, and cocked legs unleash a geyser. Every owner declares they are a "pa" or "ma" to their companion and show off with vehemence how handsome, how obedient, how attentive, and how faithful their hounds are. Faithfulness is the number one reason for keeping a dog. How desperately people need faithfulness. Even cheats and philanderers cannot stomach infidelity in another man or beast. In this city, you seldom spot a stray dog. Occasionally, you encounter one or two who have slipped their lead, but those who are lost will always be adopted. And then there are cats. Charming as they are, cats are without loyalty. So many of them find themselves driven out of the house.

Here are three interesting stories about dogs.

Once there was a couple who lived with the wife's mother for over a decade. After their son went to high school, the elderly lady passed away. The couple raised a dog instead. One day, they discovered its eyes bore a striking resemblance to the deceased woman. From then on, they were convinced she had been reincarnated. Another fellow told me that his father had died seven or eight years ago. Since then, he had increasingly and unnervingly recognised his pa in the dog. The gait and the twitching mouth were uncannily similar. There was, moreover, a man who claimed that his dog had narrow slit-like eyes. When members of the family were talking or engaged in some activity, the dog would stay by the wall with its head craned forward and its eyes slowly blinking at them. Its expression was all-seeing and all-knowing. The owner would say: "Go to your room and sleep. Bump the door closed behind you!" The dog groaned reluctantly in a tone that was neither falsetto nor bass. Maybe it was registering its defiance. Anyhow, it could comprehend human words even though people could not understand it. The pet could only repeat one word in an unusual tenor: "Wow! Wow!"

I pondered: what if a dog could speak the language of humans?

Spurred on by this thought, I broke out in a cold, fearful sweat. Oh heavens, if dogs were able to speak our language, what monstrosities would be unleashed. Every day we'd receive news to rock our foundations; the world would collapse completely. Just think about it. So many concealed secrets that belong to the stately world of humans would be taken from within our four walls and laid bare for the outside world to see. These might include the undignified antics of elderly men, youngsters refusing filial piety, a tornado of cursing, violent altercations, hanky-panky in the raw, money laundering, bribery, robbery, smoking dope, black market activities and manufacturing counterfeit goods, tax evasion, scheming, and ruthless tricks that could trip up the devil. People boast that they've uncovered the mysteries of nature. In fact, everybody has a mystery of their own to be uncovered – and it turns out that the dog is a most convenient whistleblower. Just like the black box on a plane or the president of a superpower who has his finger on the nuclear button, it wields a terrifying potential. Dogs are not truly faithful. They are agents who feign loyalty to infiltrate the family and poach its secrets. The upside of this situation is that we still have a harmonious society. How? Because a dog can master everything save for human speech. Could God permit canines to speak our tongue? Impossible! A dog who knows the language of man ceases to be a dog at all. No one would be prepared to have them as pets.

To conclude, dogs should not be allowed to speak our language. Never, ever, period.

Bald Head

The hairs on some people's heads are like bamboo shoots, springing forth wildly in all directions. I've noted that those who have a bald head are certain to have a prosperous moustache. For decades, ever since the leader of the New China refused to sport a moustache, facial hair fell out of fashion with image-conscious gentlemen. While the tobacco industry thrived, receiving a close shave at the barbershop became the norm, with deleterious effect on the market for personal razors and foam. But more and more bald headed people have also emerged. Experts in land reclamation can turn wilderness and barren mountains into lush green plots, but they are powerless to awaken a single follicle on their own bare scalps. The contradiction between head hair and moustaches is that while the one which should grow does not, the one that shouldn't runs riot. It is like the "socialist seedling" and the "capitalist grass" in the period of the Gang of Four.

Four years ago, my head was thick with black hair. I paid little attention to how much hair mattered in the lives of others and saw it as troublesome. My friends would thrust their fingers into my mane to see if there were bird's eggs in there. That summer though, it began to fall out. When I awoke in the morning, I would find fallen strands stuck to the pillow. I would mock myself by musing: "Did a woman lay her head down there last night?" That was until one day, when washing my hair, I found a clump of it floating on the water. Anxiety-ridden, I consulted the doctor and started to douse my head with growth-stimulating tonic. Nervously, I embarked on a series of remedies for the problem, but nothing had any effect. Eventually, I became a baldy.

The story of my becoming a baldy is neither an unprecedented nor isolated phenomenon. Patches of hair remained on the back of my head and temples, but the middle hollowed out like a flat ice rink. The sides, where there was still coverage, dried out and grew wrinkled like the cables in an iron wire fence. At the same time, my moustache darkened, thickened and became stiffer. If I skipped shaving for only one day, my face would be unrecognisable. The head was transforming into the face and the face into the head.

Once I became a baldy, the *feng shui* of my head altered. In other's eyes, I was no longer my former self. Assuming a shy air, I was reluctant to attend social functions. "Damn it!" I thought. "The world is in the grip of desertification and the process has spread to my head." I sank into a miserable state. From then on, I could only feel a loathing for lions, and quickly developed a fondness for hats. Wearing a hat in the summertime though was a case of *the more you try to hide, the more you're completely exposed*. Those who hadn't paid attention to my head before, now realised I was a baldy. Friends who delighted in poking fun at me in crowded places or before pretty ladies would say: "How many do you have left? Give me a single hair. I'll auction it off." I can tell you firsthand: your head is not your backside. You can't conceal it with clothing and keep it private. I reasoned I should simply lay my ugliness bare, and so went out with my forlorn scalp uncovered. In the eyes of others, my helplessness was transformed into something frank and positively charming. People become more attractive when they are charming you. Half a year has now passed and my bald head is no longer headline news. Instead, it is part of the furniture. Everyone now thinks that I was predestined to be a baldy, and the strange thing is that it didn't happen sooner. To my surprise, I found that there are reasons behind and advantages to having a bald head.

Three explanations for my bald head are:

1. According to folk theory: "Talented men are never top heavy." This theory was the conclusion of generations of empirical evidence. So, this means I'm smart.
2. Geologists have addressed how: "Grass never grows on mountains with rich mineral deposits." From this standpoint, mine is no ordinary head.
3. Women often have long hair, so this is a symbol of femininity. For a long time, mankind has obviously been feminised. A bald head is the counterpoint to this process.

God has endowed me with a mission of masculinity and the heavens are invested in my great duty. If I didn't become bald, who would?

The ten great advantages of being bald are:

1. Saving money on washing and grooming.
2. There are no little pigtails (or shortcomings) for others to tug on.
3. Knowing readily when it is hot and cold.
4. Lice are visible at first sight.
5. You are streamlined: ready to go into battle at any time.

6. Having a monk's tonsure is a sign of compassion.
7. Unable to sport the ancient "queue" braid: you cannot be labelled a pariah.
8. When you're angry, there is no hair to stand on end and push off your hat.
9. Living out your last years like a turtle.
10. Never having your unwashed hair mistaken for mould.

Nowadays, I sing a little ditty that celebrates my baldness:

Baldy:
Your mottled skin
Is smooth and slippery,
Like a painted gourd.
Without one hair,
Watermelon, bulb, or silken ball,
Shine bright on the world like a moon!

When I sing this song, I think: "What under the heavens is impossible? Hah, as long as there is a moon in the sky I can give off some radiance of my own.

On 15th March, a big group of bald-headed friends and I walked along the streets, our follicly-challenged state in full view. There were beauties drifting about like clouds. Amidst their surprise, they admired the mature self-confidence of us menfolk. They all jammed in to have their picture taken with us. We do not prohibit photography, though we ask that the nobility of a hairless man's head be respected; one can look, but never touch.

On Smoking

Smoking mimics eating, without the crass process of digestion. It is a form of connoisseurship on a par with art appreciation and fine cuisine. Like the bed chambers in the imperial palace, the stun guns used by police officers, and the tranquillisers used by insomniacs, it exists to be used by the few. Nowadays, there are far too many smokers and something must be done.

Asthmatics should be forbidden from smoking. They have so much pent-up phlegm that when they smoke they hack, giving cigarettes a bad reputation. Women should quite clearly be prohibited from smoking, since tobacco belongs to the element of fire and the female sex to the element of water. The two cannot logically coexist. Physicians should be banned on penalty of a prison sentence on account of extreme hypocrisy. Ditto the penalty for gentlemen with lengthy facial hair. Have you ever seen hay being stored in a chimney?

In an ideal world, only a tiny minority would still be permitted to smoke. They would be allowed to live like the Buddha. All day long, censers in front of his statue exhale perfumed clouds, so we can assume he is a fellow smoker. Smokers can also get together with the skunk, which secretes until the stench in the warren proves unbearable. Nicotine addicts can keep their secret together with the turtles. The turtle smokes until its shell is stained sallow. They can whinny with the donkeys. Both tuck their pipes about their waists when not in use, but the donkey's is humongous.

I am a smoker. I was born in the Year of the Dragon. Smoke clouds circulate around this dragon. I have a principle of refusing cigarettes to others; I would rather give them money. It is better to share money than hoard it. Tobacco is a kind of loyal retainer who would rather he himself burn to death. Thus, one should not offer it too freely. I firmly believe that man is the product of his environment. Chinese people should smoke Chinese cigarettes. Local people should smoke locally produced tobacco. I've stuck to the Shaanxi-made Monkey King brand for years.

A couplet inscribed on the architraves of a temple in Hangzhou reads:

Whether through fate or luck, persist in your life slowly
Whether for money or for fame, sit here and then leave.

In the midst of a busy life, why should people simply sit down? Sit down and smoke.

Walking Into the Future, Alone

Many people claim they are lonely. But those who say this out loud are likely not. Loneliness is not a matter of being abandoned or given the cold shoulder. Rather, it comes from lacking close pals or from being grossly misunderstood. Someone who is genuinely lonely will not mention it. Instead they heave long sighs like beasts.

Struggling people will find each other; ordinary people congregate with the purpose of becoming strong. Just like a pupa metamorphosing into a moth, once this change is complete, they promptly lose any original drive to fulfil their desire. Monarchs, as well as celebrities, have been through this process. For the super-rich, making money is a vacant sort of profession, just like a wild boar spreading its seed without any need for love.

I have met plenty of melancholy, sullen types. I have also met people with weird tattoos and bizarrely dyed hair. They put on an air of being lonely. This is not true loneliness but eccentricity. They want to be like wheat in June, shooting out ears when they have grown only a foot high. Their grain is no bigger than the head of a fly.

There are lonely people in every walk of life. I met one in the literary field. He was famous all over China, and the amount of slander spouted about him could blot out the sky or cover the earth. However, he never responded to comments about his work – regardless of whether he was being flattered or trampled upon, he carried on his daily life and writing. I knew that he was lonely.

One day, I approached him and said: "Sir, just think. When everyone else is coveting a bowl of prized meat, you snatch it and run away. How can you avoid being attacked by all sides?"

After hearing my words, he said nothing, nor did he stop to talk or shake hands with me. All of a sudden, his face was drenched with tears.

I chased after him, alarmed.

When I caught up with him, he retorted: "I'm not lonely." And with those words, he left.

I had failed; I thought we could become bosom buddies. Why so many tears? Did he really mean: "I'm not lonely"?

One year later, this same writer published another book. Whilst reading it, I found this sentence: "Great saints behave prosaically; great people act cautiously." I finally understood: the world is never quick to make somebody feel lonely but communal living requires a kind of balance. Jealousy triggers slander, homicide, humiliation, and other types of persecution. If you do not stand out from the crowd, you remain common. If you toil on and on, others can no longer catch up with or surpass you. They are then compelled to worship and applaud you, exalting you as some divine being. Those who are divine are truly lonely.

It is extremely hard for a man walking towards loneliness to accept the pity and sympathy of others.

Asparagus Fern

Almost a month has passed since I left behind my asparagus fern and came to make some purchases in the teeming city. Within the space of this month, the pace of time seems to have grown somehow hesitant. Seized with a feeling of being enveloped, I have become stuck in this place. At night when I dream, I am transported back to see my asparagus fern.

  Last spring when I went to visit a friend at Tianjing Mountain, it turned out my host had a penchant for flowers. His courtyard was awash with red, white and purple. Nonetheless, the first thing that caught my eye was a potted asparagus fern set among the blooms. It was still very tender and had only a single stem. Its posture was gently slanted as though half awake and half in a stupor. I drew near to the fern with an attitude of tender pity but could not bring myself to stroke it. It danced gracefully in the exhalations of my breath and showed off the fine delicacy of its shadows. It had a dream-like sweetness. I could not refrain from uttering: "Is this a paean of poetry?" The host eagerly expressed his agreement about the plant, before handing it over as a gift. From that moment, I was the custodian of this sprite and it assumed pride of place on my desk, becoming the fifth treasure of the study after my writing brush, ink, paper and inkstone. The fern was a thing of wonder. Every night as I became tired from writing, I sat transfixed. The melting moonlight seeped quietly through the latticed window, as the fern flourished with grace. Its elongated frond shone bright and dark like *yin* and *yang*. Peace flooded my heart and soul. All superfluous desires were vanquished; my mind was too full of green purity and contentment. In a split second, I was convinced that the creatures of the deep night had disappeared apart from me. I too might sprout wings and soar to join them in the nocturnal ether.

After escorting me through winter and spring, she began to develop new shoots and leaves. Every day the plant grew larger. No longer a lone stem, it now possessed three or four and held its container beneath a sumptuous canopy. Where had she been spirited from? She appeared to purify men's minds – might she save my soul? When I was happy, she channelled my joy through her every swaying limb. When I was downcast, she would decoct my gloom into lighter shadows. Then I began to prepare my ink and pens for creative work in front of her. People say that my articles abound in passion and grace. She deserves the credit for this, since her essence meanders through every line. How phenomenal it has been. In this new world, the fern was my soulmate. I could no longer tear myself away from her.

But I found myself bidding farewell to the plant to travel to the teeming city. She was left in the care of a neighbouring family.

I wondered: "Will these people nurture her? They are so slovenly. Will they remember to move her into the sunshine in the morning and carry her back in the evening? They might do that for a day or two, but then they would probably lose patience."

They might place her directly under the window, where she would be manhandled by the wind and daubed with dust. Her leaves would become withered and fall off one by one, floating out into the pigsty or byre, where they would be ravaged by animals. I also fear they might not water her every day. They might spare only half a bowl of cold tea or dirty dishwater. How will my plant bear this? She needs to be neither too wet nor too dry. When the sun is setting, a bowl of water should be served. The water should not be entirely pure clean water nor full of fertiliser. Rather it should have been stored in a bottle for a long time together with extract of horse hoof. This refreshment should be dribbled in from a height.

I am at a loss to understand my behaviour. How could I have entrusted my dear plant to this suffering?

I have not yet made all my purchases in town, so I cannot go back. Made feeble with worry, I head across town to the flower market to see what their ferns are like. Plentiful as they are, none has such a natural grace as mine. They are poor and insipid by comparison. My mind is swamped with pride and longing for her. At night, I curl up in bed and, half asleep, form an impression of her sashaying delicately into my dream. My visitor does not look like an asparagus fern, but a girl. Her beauty overwhelms me. She leans against the door, her slender shoulders trembling as she sobs.

"Why are you crying?" I ask.

"I am heartbroken. When I was born, I was loved by all, but now no one understands me. I sense only their bitter envy; I have every reason to cry." Tears trickle down from her eyes.

Oh, I understand the plight of girls like her. Their temperament is as noble as the sky, but their fate is as humble as a scrap of paper – glistening white yet easily soiled and torn.

"Why do they treat me this way?"

I smile gently: "How come you were born so pretty?"

With her eyes wide she stares at me lividly. I become very embarrassed. She suddenly blurts out: "Is that my fault? I came into this world with seemingly only one role – showing off my looks. Maybe I am fragile and weak, but I am also delicate and noble. I am headstrong. I won't stand being messed about."

I am taken aback.

"Who are you and what is your name?"

"Asparagus Fern."

"Asparagus Fern?" With a loud cry of remorse, I open my eyes and realise I was dreaming. Usually my dreams leave me feeling perplexed on waking. This one, however, touches something in me. In the silence that follows, I meditate as the reprobate I am. I know my duty. I must return and be reunited with my asparagus fern.

Talking about the Dragon in the Year of the Dragon

The Chinese people worship many things. As well as the sun and the moon, rivers, the voice, light, thunder and lightning, they also revere animals. They believe that each life is the reincarnation of a past existence. Thus, according to the Chinese zodiac, people born in a particular year belong to an animal sign: including the rat, cow, tiger, rabbit, snake, horse, sheep, monkey, rooster, dog, and the pig. These animals take turns on duty, presiding over all the others. A dozen years forms a complete cycle or *samsara*. Those people whose zodiac year has cycled back around may look worried and cautious. It is told that, if the first days of the year – with all their potential challenges – proceed smoothly, then all else will follow likewise. But the reverse is also true. This is a kind of strategic pass, a threshold that must be negotiated successfully. Those marking their year wear a red belt and traditionally lay out a spread of liquor and dishes in celebration. Should one good thing transpire, it will accumulate a second, then a third, and so on. Thereafter, should one bad thing occur, the ill fortune will be split. The trouble will shrink in time, like nuclear half-lives, becoming smaller and smaller until it disappears altogether.

  I was born in the Year of the Dragon. The hours of the dragon are 7–9am. The new century will chime in to the reign of the dragon when I'm forty-nine years old – a crucial stage on the route to reaching a century. Several days ago, when I gathered with friends, they said they would hold a party for me. As soon as they expressed these sentiments, they headed to the shops to purchase red cord to be woven into the ceremonial belt. They discussed booking tables at a luxury hotel. Their fussing made me realise that he who enjoys the year of his animal does not necessarily have to suffer ill fortune, but may instead enjoy an unremittingly good time. Why the red belt? It is to declare that this year the god of my life will be on duty. It is like becoming a trial judge, being promoted to the position of chair, or the captain of a football team – sporting his red armband proudly. From the standpoint of Chinese Confucianism, the person on duty is raised to be powerful and mighty. Nevertheless, they have social responsibilities. They should avoid flippancy, arrogance and presumptuousness. "Great saints behave prosaically; great people act cautiously." Only in this way are these public servants capable of serving the people. Of course, you must spare no effort in performing your duty and, what is more, think through all plans for the year at least twice. In addition, you should lay the table; you should be the one to host and treat others. For, on the one hand, people may come over to cheer and congratulate. On the other, as an official you should be ready to console them.

In the minds of Chinese people, the dragon reigns supreme and almighty. Every emperor declared himself not only "the Son of Heaven" but also the "True Dragon". In accordance with folk customs, ordinary people feel overly proud at having been born in the Year of the Dragon. While an American athlete is overjoyed to wear the stars and stripes, we Chinese sing a song entitled "Offspring of the Dragon". Now, in this new era of fire-breathing, the dragon is on duty from 7–9am. What great fortune to have such an industrious early riser to rule. This is the will of heaven. The country is going to be rejuvenated. A Chinese Millennium Monument has been built in Beijing. The leaders of the central government attended the opening ceremony in the chilly evening. The spectacle was magnificent. All over China people hung lamps and colourful ribbons. They constructed dragon platforms and hoisted dragon lanterns. Whatever they did, they went to town. According to news reports, in some provinces calligraphers used giant brushes to write out the character for "dragon" across their local squares. The letters stretched for 100 metres. On witnessing these marvels, those born in the Year of the Dragon were indeed overjoyed. The children and grandchildren of the dragon, though varied in age, all looked on these grand ceremonies as if they were their own birthday party.

What logic lay behind the compilation of the Chinese zodiac? Why is it that the rat, cow, tiger, rabbit, snake, horse, sheep, monkey, rooster, dog, and the pig were chosen and not the lion, the bear or the elephant? For a long time, I have been confused about this. Of the group, eleven are real animals. But the dragon stands out as special by virtue of its mythological status. Chinese people respect animals, but they only revere the dragon – a composite of many creatures and images – as a totem. This suggests a keenness for symbolism without analytical scrutiny, an aesthetic propensity for elegance and grace without words of explanation. In their art, the Chinese strive for clarity and harmony. This can indeed be perceived as cathartic in effect whilst eschewing the shock value of Western tragedies.

Everybody talks about the cultural differences between East and West. Nowadays, American culture holds sway over the rest of the world. More and more people, especially scholars who follow the trends, favour parroting Western viewpoints to attack the Chinese. They compare Western cream to Chinese cabbage. They don't recognise that although flesh-eating animals are larger and stronger than those that graze, a tiny flea still sucks blood. An elephant is a colossus, yet it eats grass. A problem rears its head: the dragon is an imaginary, Frankenstein animal – a collage of numerous others. If we regard this synthetic being as a totem, it will resonate with solemnity and grandeur. But out in the natural world, if you are a tiger cub you must grow like a tiger, if you are a lion cub you must grow like a lion. If you insist on growing both this way and that, you will degenerate into something small and grotesque like a lizard, a chicken, a gecko or a salamander. Anything borrowed from a foreign culture ought to be enriching to the spirit. Our ancestors concocted this image of the dragon, but their offspring have fallen into a regrettable habit. Whenever they invent something new, they take their inspiration from how the dragon was formed. They fuse together disparate sources and while doing so, they make many thoughtless mistakes.

The dragon has been around in China since antediluvian times. And yet the collective impression is that the dragon was first embroidered upon the Qing Dynasty national flag. Now, when the Chinese discuss national tradition, we don't trace our spiritual fountainhead back so very far; we only look back to the effete dynasties of the Ming and Qing. As a result, when we celebrate the Year of the Dragon, those who participate in the dragon and lion dance and those who beat drums and gongs wear neither the apparel of the Han and Tang dynasties, nor even a Sun Yat-sen suit. They all dress in the vulgar colours and style of the Ming and Qing periods, allowing us only the small mercy of omitting the dangling, greasy queue. Look around: how meagre and withered is the image of the dragon in modern times.

Originally, the dragon was fictitious, but those artists who painted dragons and artisans who crafted their likenesses made it more concrete, as if some really existed below the heavens. They became like the cat on the *kang* or the dog guarding the back door. I appreciate the ancient dragon carvings, their combinations of fish, tiger, horse, snake, deer and pig features. The dragons on jade ware, bronze tripods and weapons unearthed from the Western Zhou and Warring States times are all very simple but display their shape and power in accordance with the artefact they decorate. They exude extraordinary imagination. By contrast, the contemporary dragon has been vulgarised. People call a snake or a pig a "dragon". Their imagination and creativity have abandoned them entirely. Day after day, the grandeur of the national totem has been eroded. The citizens of the dragon nation heave a deep sigh. Even I – a son of the Year of the Dragon – feel angry over this.

Several days ago, I ran into a friend who is apt to mock others. He used to call me "Little Jia". Years later, he calls me "Old Jia".

Now that he has begun to address me as "Sir", he said, "Sir, it's high time that you rode off on the clouds and fog."

I replied: "Is that so? But you're older than I am. I should call you 'Sir'."

"Then how should I address you?"

I told him that we could call each other "your lordship". An archaic form of address, but a good one. When a senior addresses a junior like this, it is meant to show deference. It also serves to praise the virtue of a gentleman.

He said: "That's nice, Jia, your lordship. How gallant you

are. Next year is the Year of the Dragon. If you prosper, don't forget to take us lowly dogs and chickens up to the heavens with you."

"I will try to remember, but let me first warn you: a devil is at large in the world. His name is Mr Smart Arse."

Even though our ribbing was good natured, I consulted several dictionaries for the definition of "dragon" once home. I came to feel that people born in the Year of the Dragon do indeed bear its character. My ailing body has miraculously transformed into that of a dragon. When I found myself a sick man, I first admitted myself as an inpatient, but on entering the ward and settling in with my daily drip, I decided that from 31st December 1999 I would leave my illness behind with the passing millennium. For the last thirty years, I have been the famously ill writer amongst the literati. My physical and spiritual malaise has rendered life too fatiguing and arduous; I have been in hibernation like a hermit, living sensibly and without the assistance of alms. When the New Year comes, I will rise up and show myself, harnessing the wind and the rain and turning the rivers and the seas upside down.

It is New Year's Eve and loud music fills the air across Xi'an. People crowd into the streets like ants to enjoy the new millennium. A number of friends – fellow dragons – gather in my home. Slowly, I write out the following characters: "Fate offered by heaven remains long and prosperous." These were the words marked by the royal seal when Qin Shihuang unified China, around two centuries before the birth of Christ.

I say: "Whoah, two millennia have passed. The characters of the royal seal were created by dragons!"

The City of Xi'an

I have been living in the city of Xi'an for twenty years; I dare not say that this city belongs to me or think what I contribute to it; but two decades ago, when I was still in the countryside of southern Shaanxi, I dreamt about a tree. This ancient tree was not so tall, and it had a noticeable hole.

There are forests blanketing the mountains of my hometown, but I could not find such a tree there. When I was first a resident of the city, I discovered it on the street; identical to the one in my dream. I inspect the tree every year, so I know that it continues to grow. Its dead branches stiffen, yet new growth remains supple as a willow.

I often stare at the cast-off cicada shell lying on the cracked surface of the trunk, feeling puzzled. I wonder how many times one cicada can shed its casing. A life which entails such a metamorphosis is fascinating for this birth cannot happen without death. But where are the flying cicadas born and where do they die? At dusk, beneath the setting sun to the south of the city wall, I listen to a group of crickets sing intricate melodies in the timeworn crevices within the brickwork. In a trance, I feel that this brick is me or that I am one of the crickets, staring up at the expansive sky each night, crooning to greet every bright moon.

I am glad that Xi'an lies here in the west of China on the vast Guanzhong Plain; only in such a place could a city like this exist. I celebrate it with a folk ballad:

Loess drifts over the Qin land of eight hundred li,
Thirty million Qin folk roar out local opera,
A bowl of sticky noodles fills them with glee,
But having no pepper makes them complain.

Such a piece of doggerel may lack modern character, but backwardness per se is not tantamount to ignorance. The power it radiates, however, is neither hypocritical nor superficial. By scrutinising how people used to live, it generates a cold sort of humour. There is a movingly tragic story behind the ballad, which I cannot communicate by merely singing it. Kuafu the giant chased after the sun and died from thirst on his way to the sea. This reminds me that a few years ago, I refused an invitation from a group of people from the south of China. I was headhunted; they dangled before me offers of sumptuous hospitality. I turned them down because I love, too deeply, only Shaanxi and the city of Xi'an.

I was not born in Xi'an, but I shall die here. After my passing, my corpse will be incinerated in the crematorium; my soul will climb out of the high chimney riding on the black smoke and I shall become a cloud wandering over the city.

As new cities in this world increasingly resemble a heap of cement, how can I describe the city of Xi'an? It is well known that Xi'an was the capital of thirteen historical dynasties and how the eight waterways which wove around Chang'an endowed it with an enviable feng shui. As time has gone by, it is true that Xi'an no longer forms the political, economic and cultural centre of China. And yet the most sublime thing is that the city still abounds in ancient charm and elegance. Xi'an retains the most rarefied atmosphere of any classical metropolis across the entire world. The city wall is remarkably intact. When one stands alone on the drawbridge above the moat and raises one's head to survey the gate tower, turrets and crenellations, even the most timid of people cannot help but burst into loud, passionate rhapsodies.

The streets and lanes are geometric and symmetrical. The neatly and decently appointed residential courtyards conspire together with the iron-complexioned walkways beneath carved eaves to transport one into an ancient world. That world is populated with strong, stately horses pulling large wooden carts. Given the opportunity, one could begin to note thousands of street names from within the city: Examination Hall Gate (Gongyuanmen), Scholars' Academy Gate (Shuyuanmen), Bamboo-ware Market (Zhubashi), Glazed-ware Street (Liulijie), Military Training Ground Gate (Jiaochangmen), Imperial Attire Inspection Gate (Duanlimen), Charcoal Street (Tanshijie), Wheat Straw Street (Maixianjie), Carters' Inn Lane (Chejiaxiang), Northern Oil Lane (Beiyouxiang).

One suddenly feels that history is not so distant. Even when an unsanitary fly rushes before you, it is tempting to think it too bears the imprint of the Han or Tang dynasties. Modern entertainment is customarily staged in large deluxe theatres, cinemas or song and dance halls. At the foot of the city wall, where mosses form a carpet like ancient coins, there will always be spectators watching the most timeworn local Qin opera, shadow displays, and puppet shows. These performers are not professional actors or artists; they simply dabble for pleasure. Someone puts on a performance, someone else is sure to appreciate it. Performers and audiences alike find an outlet for unburdening their pent-up pride. A seam of historical memory surges through the daily lives of Xi'an people. You may, therefore, be able to understand why among those utensils used by food vendors on the street, the hefty, thick-sided vessel is referred to as a *haiwan* ("bowl as vast as the sea").

Have you seen people performing folk operas or stilt walking during festivals, as they do in Xi'an? They carry apricot-yellow flags and banners and blunderbusses, and beat out striking drum rhythms. The local dialect is fascinating. If written out phonetically, it's clearly constructed from the most elegant words from classical Chinese: folks do not speak of "carrying" (*bao*) a child but of "conveying" (*xie*) it; where their mouths cannot detect flavour they do not say "tasteless" (*mei wei*) but "numbed senseless" (*gua*); even when they curse they say "skedaddle" (*bi*) instead of "bugger off" (*gun*).

In case of casual callers – and regardless of whether the homeowner is an artist, a worker, a clerk, or a self-employed peddler – the Xi'an living room must display elaborately decorated scrolls and paintings. Likewise, tables must be festooned with choice specimens of ancient ceramics. In their daily lives, locals are expected to have at least a basic understanding of calligraphy, painting, and how to preserve cultural relics. In aesthetics, men admire black and white, while women prefer striking red and dazzling green. The people here are straightforward and honest, uninhibited about how they express joy and woe. They are taciturn yet demonstrative, savour silence, are agile of thought, worship wisdom, and deplore wiliness. They have a heroic vigour untainted by trivia and affectionate display.

Xi'an has no shortage of high-tech personnel. Many world-famous mathematicians and physicists were born here. However, among the populace there are still plenty who are familiar with the ancient classic, *Book of Changes*. These people can observe celestial phenomena and admire the *feng shui* of the landscape; they can foretell the future and exercise telepathy. One should never underestimate the older man who drinks alone in the corner of the inn or the white-haired, wizened woman. Perhaps they are learned masters with incomparable gifts.

In the early morning at the vegetable market, you will see people clutching blocks of tofu in their hands, chitchatting about local news. The residents of Xi'an have no need to waste time on state and international affairs. Nonetheless, they have an innate instinct for caring about others. This has been passed on to them by their ancient capital. Instead of mocking the proverbial "man of Qi who feared the heavens would tumble down", they sympathise. Some people have solemnly proposed that a huge statue of him be erected in the centre alongside Zhang Qian, the pioneer of the Silk Road. These would become twin emblems of the city.

The aura of ancient Chinese history permeates Xi'an. But its role as ancient relic doesn't prevent it forming a fresh and lively symbol of China.

Pottery Figures

After the Terracotta Army was unearthed, I observed people pointing at Shaanxi folk working in Beijing and saying: "Look! You're a terracotta warrior. Alike as two peas in a pod." What they've said is correct. Man is a product of his environment. His appearance evolves incrementally over time. I am a native and long-term resident of Shaanxi, found in the northwest of China where the land is steep and the winds bracing. Locals relish making food from wheat flour. They are stout-waisted with broad shoulders, wide faces and brawny bodies. As people meander in a crowd, I cast my eye over what is familiar to me. According to historical records, Shaanxi folk are "strong-willed and simple-minded". This strength and simplicity likely refer to Shaanxi males. Nowadays, this province is loudly acclaimed all over China for its beauties. What were the physical attributes of Shaanxi people in dynasties gone by? We have no photographs of our ancestors, so I must turn to the museum's pottery figures to understand.

The earliest surviving work of figurative pottery consists of only a man's head. It resembles the lid of some lost container; its eyes gaze up at the sky while its mouth is a little ajar. This is a prehistoric Shaanxi person. We don't have those tiny eyes now. Its mouth is opened slightly because that was the age in which the clay ocarina was invented. The people wanted to channel the gravid sound of the earth. How wonderful it is that their mouths were slightly open; human beings had already realised their place in this world. They knew everything but never boasted. Shaanxi folk look down on the silver-tongued. Until now, they have been loath to listen to the "twittering" of southerners, the "greasy lips" of Beijingers and the "slippery tongues" of Tianjin.

When the Great Qin Dynasty was established, the Terracotta Army was cast. Young and old, male and female alike – all know of the might and grandeur of the earthenware warriors. The pottery horses are almost life-size, and the human figures were surely modelled to scale. How great, then, were the ancestors of the Shaanxi people. It is only a little embarrassing that the warriors have elongated midriffs and stumpy legs. But on second thoughts, this perhaps made them better equipped for ancient warfare. The history books record that "the Great Qin had an army of wolves and tigers". Tigers' legs are short. If they had the legs of an egret, they would be better equipped to become Japanese kabuki dancers. Shaanxi people traditionally adore martial arts. One of their outstanding characteristics is that those who excel at this skill, keep it to themselves. The facial expressions of these pottery figures are peaceful, almost to the point of ineptitude. This could be what the history books meant by "simple-minded". On the other hand, when their patience was tested, they rose up and conquered the six rival states. From how these forces sprang into action, people can well imagine too what the "strong will" mentioned in the annals was.

These descriptions refer to Shaanxi males during the Qin Dynasty. What about Shaanxi women? The kneeling terracotta warriors have their hair bound into knots at the back of their heads. Their faces are delicate and comely and the way their hands are pressed against their knees conveys an attitude of calmness and quiet. When they were first excavated, they were regarded as "she-warriors". As more warriors of this type were unearthed, it was discovered that each of them shared a burial pit with a steed. They sported moustaches. It became obvious that these were also male – stable hands of the underworld. If a stable hand could look like this, imagine the women! There are no pottery figurines of females. Was that because Qin men were chauvinists or were they unwilling to send their womenfolk out to toil? We don't know. Nowadays, women from the south are reluctant to marry Shaanxi men. They complain that Shaanxi men can't cook, launder or tailor clothes. They are incapable of minding their own children. Whereas, Shaanxi men will curse the southern men for sending their women to work barefoot to plant rice seedlings in the paddy or haul manure along the field terraces. Whoever has the right idea, they must beg to differ.

During the Han Dynasty, more warriors appeared. There were warriors who clutched shields, figures modelled in profile, and cavalrymen. The abundance of earthenware replicas signifies that this was a civilised era, since it suggests that fewer slaves were being buried alive with their masters. The figures with shields and a sideways aspect are all very thin. Some are seated, others stand. They appear serene and poised in their manner, plain and delicate in dress, and wear friendly expressions – the embodiment of feminine tenderness. The Han and Tang dynasties were the most powerful periods in Chinese history. The beginning of the Han Dynasty marked a period of rehabilitation; it was a peaceful era. Our ancestors at that time focused on pragmatic living, without ostentatiousness. Sometimes the strong will of the Shaanxi people exploded like a scroll unfurling to reveal a hidden dagger. But at other times, they cultivated their power like a marathon. Among the folk sculpture of the Han Dynasty, the "eight cut" carvings are especially renowned. Their masterful simplicity is well known, with the benchmark being the stonework at the Maoling Mausoleum.

These days, the sublimity of Shaanxi is displayed not only in architecture, clothing, food and handicrafts, but also in everyday speech and etiquette. Shaanxi folk are not hesitant by nature. They dislike a fuss being made over trivial matters, and when they find themselves on the backfoot, they stay silent no matter how they are lambasted. You may think that they are like the water used to feed pasture – spent and irretrievable – but you are wrong. The irrigation percolates through the soil with every intention of spurting forth again in the future.

The lion's share of warriors has been dug out of tombs from the Han Dynasty. Three thousand were found in a single tomb at Yang Family Bend in Xianyang. They are smaller than the Qin warriors. Even so, forty per cent of the troops are cavalrymen. In the Han Dynasty, Shaanxi people were adept equestrians. It is a pity that even the local Guanzhong strain of horse is almost extinct. The unrestrained robustness of the steeds has been lost in the native folk too. To this day, Shaanxi people seldom buy clothes from Shanghai and are unwilling to travel in the company of those from the south.

Shaanxi folk are not directly descended from the ancient Han people alone. Starting from the Qin Dynasty, their blood was already becoming diluted. Year in, year out, they engaged in battle with nomadic tribes. And yet the blood and culture of our ancestors intermingled with our nomadic rivals. Many military soldiers feature among the pottery figures of the Wei and Jin, and the Northern and Southern

Dynasties. A number of these are of the Hun race. If you observe closely, you will note the riders who carry a bugle, the warriors who pound rice and even the human-faced, tomb-guarding animals with their large noses and deep-set eyes. Some of them have wide, determined faces. Others appear handsome, with their neat eyebrows or the distinctive Yunnan and Sichuan hairstyles. History books mention that "five nomadic tribes disturbed ancient China", when in fact they disturbed only Shaanxi. On account of their prodigious hybridisation, the people of Shaanxi seem robust and powerful in build, tolerant in nature and, despite being easy to cheat, would never cheat another.

Owing to the hybridisation during the Southern and Northern dynasties, from the Sui Dynasty to the beginning of the Tang Dynasty, China regained its prosperity. Hence, the golden age in the middle Tang Dynasty through which we can witness the glory of our ancestors.

* * *

The Heavenly King

Apart from the mighty figure of the "Heavenly King", the small ghosts underneath his feet are somewhat unusual. He isn't frustrated from being trodden on. Instead, he is quietly spoiling for a chance at retaliation. This reminds me of the character of present-day Shaanxi people. They are of the sort who clearly know they are no match for their rivals, but still lunge forward, their faces becoming bloodied.

* * *

The tricolour ladies-in-waiting

With full-moon faces and plump waists tapering downwards, these women show off a voluptuous beauty, their long skirts cascading to the floor. They are healthy in build and vigorous in spirit. It was the trend at that time to equate power with beauty and vice versa. For Shaanxi women of today, the two phenomena still co-exist. On the one hand they remain calm, bashful and full of grace. On the other, they are outgoing, warm, and unrestrained. This is perhaps the legacy of the Han and Tang dynasties.

* * *

Woman on horseback

The woman appears with bared chest and arms and the "horse" is in fact a zebra. She is regal and alluring, exuding the air of an aristocratic lady in eighteenth-century Europe.

* * *

Woman seated before a dressing table

Her skirts are rolled up high with her underwear on view. The sleeves of her blouse are turned back and her tricolour dress is strikingly gaudy. Before the looking glass, she is pinning a flower into her hair. As more female statuettes have been recovered from tombs, we can observe how there were once more than 140 different hairstyles. The Tang Dynasty not only worshipped power but revelled in showing it off. All the men flaunted their power, while all the women showcased their beauty. What a self-confident era!

The Shaanxi people's habit of keeping fit is apparent in a set of hunting warriors on horseback. The humour and jocosity of Shaanxi people is evident from the chatting and singing figurines. From the earthenware figures of Kunlun mountain dwellers and the Hunnish equestrians, riders of couchant camels and horse minders, we can discern that Shaanxi people are open, broadminded and receptive towards foreign cultures. Another troupe of seven female musicians are in high spirits as they balance on the backs of dromedaries. It's clear why Shaanxi folk song and opera have been so popular across China.

* * *

The Qin Dynasty is gone, the Han Dynasty has passed, the Tang Dynasty is no more. The capital has migrated northwards and eastwards, further away from this province. In turn, the power of the economic, political and cultural centre has waned. This is a matter of the greatest pity for Shaanxi people.

A pottery likeness of women bearing gifts has been unearthed from Bai Family Ridge in Ankang. They are delicate and slim, clad in unisex-style overcoats. Male warriors were found too, wearing three-piece outfits. By the Song Dynasty, gone was the abundance of luxury and self-confidence. Advancing into the Ming Dynasty, there were sometimes more than three hundred ceramic figures unearthed from a single tomb. Despite their outward magnificence, the stewards and the guard of honour are without any inner spirit. They are just helplessly obedient shells. There is something about the Ming and Qing dynasties that corroded the

Shaanxi people, creating their modern-day shortcomings. These eras founded Shaanxi clumsiness, pedanticism and a brutal kind of honesty.

Every time I visit the pottery figures in the provincial museum, I witness the passing of one generation after another of Shaanxi forebears. Each period has its own unique aesthetics and ideology. The nuances have served to nurture the appearance and nature of the Shaanxi people. The creation, development and decline of the pottery figures has been a source of both contentment and unease. For more than two thousand years, they have bequeathed these emotions to the Chinese nation.

Shaanxi folk are a microcosm of Chinese national history. The Reform and Opening-up of China policy started in the late twentieth century, but because it is located in the northwest of China, Shaanxi has fallen behind other provinces. Its economic backwardness has given outsiders an excuse to look down upon its inhabitants. We should take stock of what has happened in the past in order to foretell the future. What are we lucky to possess and what do we lack? The key ingredient for economic development and cultural renaissance is not the geographical environment but human beings themselves. The ancestors of the Shaanxi people were the seed of the dragon. The offspring of this seed cannot turn out to be fleas. When many of my friends have visited this province, my greatest pleasure has been to lead them to the Terracotta Army and to take them to see the stone statues at the Maoling Mausoleum, together with the Tang Dynasty frescoes. I've asked them: "In Chinese history, why was it that the Qin, the Han and the Tang were so powerful? It's because they built their capitals in Shaanxi. Shaanxi people were their bedrock. The Song,

Yuan, Ming and Qing never enjoyed such strong central power. Shaanxi people lost out in this process too." My friends readily concur with my sentiments but take exception to how I express them, my neck and face flushing red with enthusiasm. They respond: "You've turned an interesting colour – behold, the latest terracotta warrior!"

Wall Paintings

The yellow earth of Shaanxi lies thick. Deep below the surface, you will find the abundant tombs of the Great Tang Dynasty. Only a few have been excavated, including Princess Yongtai, Prince Zhanghuai, Prince Yide, Princess Fang Ling, Li Shou and Zhang Hao. To a great number of rare treasures, add more than three hundred square metres of tomb fresco discoveries – all now on display in the basement of the Shaanxi History Museum. These murals are different from the specimens in the Dunhuang Caves. The tomb occupants all belonged in some way to the ranks of royalty and wanted to prolong their nobility after death. The wall paintings are thus composed of ladies-in-waiting and their steeds. Imagine what a rich, contented existence was to be had back then.

The day I visited the murals it was scorching outside, but rather cool in the underground gallery. As the door to the collection swung open, I felt so timid, I almost dared not step over the threshold. Whenever you watch costume dramas with historical characters stalking back and forth across the set, you feel a barrier; history is history and I am who I am.

Peeking into the subterranean hall from the entrance, I felt like a country bumpkin spying on the workings of the royal palace. "The beauties are banked up like clouds" is a phrase used to describe our present-day streets. Even if the beauties on the streets are banked up like clouds, they lack the graceful delicacy and simplicity of the clouds. It is always reported that "Tang beauties were plump". This now arouses some scepticism: should the concubine Yang Yuhuan be counted as a genuine beauty?

The palace ladies-in-waiting depicted in the mural are tall, with elongated noses, almond-shaped eyes, large bosoms and broad hips. They wear gowns which sweep the ground; they are the picture of finesse and charm. Their steeds have rangy posteriors; their legs painted slender and steely-strong. We can tell that woman and horse co-exist harmoniously. The spirit of the Tang Dynasty was enthusiastic and cosmopolitan, unrestrained and bold. Only in the present has western Europe come to enjoy a comparable combination of a prosperous economy, an emancipated culture, and the merging of races. The Chinese are always surprised by the athleticism of western European women and call them "mighty foreign mares", not realising that this phenomenon was seen in the early Tang Dynasty too. Hence, we lament how the power of the nation slid so drastically after the end of the Tang. The more we were invaded, the further we migrated to the south, adopting an increasingly closed mindset. Our race gradually became atrophied and our physiques grew frailer. Some people argue that the "purity" of the Han ethnicity is preserved only in the residents of Singapore and the remotest south-east corner of China. That may well be so. While the Tang were said to prize plumpness as a sign of beauty, what they cared for most was power. The era of those horses is sliding into the ever more distant past. In our poems we praise dainty donkeys and beaten down oxen. Mules are to be found on the plains, though these are only the vassals of horses.

How I adore Tang beauties.

Finally, I walked into the basement hall, heading to its depths. Painted in 593 AD and visited by me only in 1997, the frescoes in Dunhuang cast a mysterious impression. But with these royal ladies-in-waiting, I noted that the contrast between then and now is not simply about dress. Their round and mellow faces, the way their hair grows, and their slim and refined bodies made me feel the breath of real people. Looking at them, I felt they were so vividly alive that I maintained a cautious sideways shuffle in their presence. I feared a collision with them. They seemed reserved yet they were busying themselves in a very organised way. Some were bearing silver salvers, others grasping lamps, and some were playing with the loose fabric of their sleeves to amuse geese, watching birds or hunting cicadas. When faced with the unfamiliar – me – they neither flattered nor were cruel. Their expressions were the picture of composure. These women, drawn from the ranks of civilians, may be dogged by loneliness, worry and anxiety. But they are still members of the royal entourage. They would look down on a rustic like me. As I regarded them as immortal beings, they filled me with a profound admiration that left me humble and inferior.

I understood then the frenzied mentality of Jia Baoyu in *Dream of the Red Chamber*. I could not help but murmur his words: "Women are made of water; men are made of mud." Look at the head lady in *Nine Palace Ladies-in-Waiting*. Her hair was bound up high and her hands were holding either end of the scarf wrapped around her shoulders. Eight others followed behind her, bearing a salver, a casket, a candlestick, a circular fan, a tall-stemmed goblet, a horsetail duster, a parcel, an S-shaped jade charm. They processed in graceful unison. Enraptured, I observed the sixth: such a timeless, peerless beauty. Her hair was twisted into a coil and a scarf enfolded her shoulders. Her dress brushed the floor. Her goblet was perfectly to scale; the ideal companion for her frame, which seemed to turn effortlessly. Her eyes were slightly lowered. Unconsciously, she broke into a smile. Her grace and elegance knew no limits. I should have addressed her tenderly as "sixth youngest sister". I firmly believed that such a noble and cultivated beauty was not a figment of the artist's imagination, but sketched with a living, breathing model before him. She must have been kept deep inside the royal palace. Even the Tang people themselves must have seldom clapped eyes on such a damsel. But at last I saw her. I saw a millennium-old beauty.

"This beauty is one thousand years old," A friend who had joined me on this visit declared.

My friend's words filled me with sorrow, but he felt consoled to think that even beauties grow old. I didn't rebuke him. Whenever people are made to consider ageing beauty, there is always a twofold response of both joy and grief. This strange attitude might have been shared by those royals and aristocrats. When they were alive, she was their chattel. When they died, they brought her along to the underworld. Their legacy for future generations was an aged beauty. All those royals and nobles were reduced to dust. Whether human or canine, not a trace was left of their outlines. And yet, these ladies remained in the murals. Their souls have been channelled into the paintings; the souls of old ghosts, buried in tombs for thousands of years. But I didn't feel the least tinge of terror. I felt very close to them, as if I knew them. As though our paths had crossed in a hotel or out on the street. I told my friend: "Now do you understand why in *Strange Tales from the Liaozhai Studio*, the talented young men are always expecting a female spirit to fly in through the window?"

After visiting the murals, I bought a facsimile of the artworks, produced by Mr Tang Changdong. I didn't want "sixth youngest sister" to be trapped in the thousand-year old palace or inside the deep tomb of the museum. Originally, that girl was drawn from the ranks of the ordinary citizenry. I wish I could truly have brought her home with me. I hung the replica in my room, hoping for her to break out. I said: "Sixth youngest sister, I won't trap you in the aristocracy. Nor do I have a gold-lined cell to hide you in. But I could offer you freedom and happiness, and allow you to be a shepherdess. Then I shall take my lead from the songwriter Wang Luobin and transform myself into a small lamb. In that way, you can gently swish your whip against my body.

The Wild Land

The terrain was originally given over to crops, then reclaimed by wild grass which reached the height of a man. Vigorous, fecund and poised. One moonlit evening, when no wind blew – and it was not yet time for the dew to settle – the blades of grass and its ripened ears stood so quietly that the sound of breathing was palpable. It sounded like seeds were scratching out through their husks in an effort to escape, or like the rustle of insects nibbling. Someone paused there in the silence for a long time, the thumping of their heart joining the raspy breath. Like the characters in *Strange Tales from the Liaozhai Studio*, the clock seemed to shift back to an ancient primeval wilderness. You could hear the gods dictating fate from afar.

The moon was clear and bright in the sky, yet with shadows etched on the surface. Was one a reflection of the wild land? On the ground, everything beyond three feet away was shrouded and chaotic. The night kept its secrets close, so liaisons were initiated only belatedly. Evading the sentry tower-like hut – used for keeping an eye on the crops – a single hungry, thirsting hand grasped hold of another hungry, thirsting hand. Ten fingers were locked together in an instant, both feeling the heat, though they shivered with cold.

A plot of black earth stretched across the eyeline of the trespasser. The soil was tender. Stepping on it felt like wearing a pair of ill-fitting, oversized shoes. The pitiful farmers had sown a row of potatoes here, but the grasses surrounding them prevented them from thriving. The tubers had not even managed to reach the size of a man's fist. The following morning, two lines of intersecting footprints remained in the soil.

Coming to the centre of the wild meadow, you could easily lose your bearings. The interlopers found themselves here, in the intense stillness. Body and soul urged them to be seated. Two rocks were planted beside them. How many years and months had passed for these expectant stones? Even they had grown frigid in their waiting. Wild grass streamed between the heavens and the earth. The man was also a blade of wild grass with a stalk to his side. They conversed about Tang poems and Song "ci" verse. The moon above their heads was plump as an expected breeze arrived. The grass bisected the pooling moonlight into strips, and it shimmered and shook. The anonymous insects groaned, spraying their unique odours. The land witnessed a repeated *petit mort* and rebirthing, then once more things were peaceful. It was awkward to detect the shadows under the moonlight, like peering into the waters of a deep well.

In a precinct as sacred as the Buddha's shrine, body and soul were fused in harmony. They understood that this plot was a portal to the future disguised in a carpet of earth.

Were undutiful farmers to blame for the influx of wild grass? It was quickly yielding swollen seeds, bursting into new life. Perhaps people would curse the undutiful farmers for this. But the fragile crops were not so strong. The wild grass thrived without the need for ploughing, fertiliser or the turning of the seasons.

People were restored to their original primitive form because of the grass. How grand and boundless was this night under moonlight.

The hardship and grief of life has produced countless regrets and ugly mistakes. Whoever can overcome these acquires good humour, no longer pinning their hopes on dreams or the next life. They may sit on the wild land as steady as the two stones. They may sit there for hundreds or thousands of years, or they may tarry there for only a short while. That would be enough.

Today there is another plot I know where the grass is sparse. It's land for growing melons, maybe also pumpkins and watermelons. The farmers are unlikely to harvest what they were expecting. The melon patch has long lay fallow. The leaves of the melon vines have turned to fetid mud, yet the vines, though withered and white, still crisscross like ropes, leaving their imprints on the ground. Walking along the grid formed by these white ropes feels akin to playing a game. One can suddenly recall the laurel on the moon, and the brave Wu Gang, who could not hack through its trunk.

But I'll not forget that the wild land did exist.

Shangluo is My Homeland

A speech delivered at the Jia Pingwa Literary Symposium, Shangluo College of Higher Education, November 2014.

Everyone insists that their own homeland is great. Myself included. Whenever Shangluo is mentioned, my eyes brighten. This isn't just an instinctive feeling, but one that wells up through all my literary works.

Although Shangluo lies in a mountainous region, standing here now, Beijing feels like a backwater, as does Shanghai. Although comparatively down-at-heel, its mountains, waterways, sunshine and air are pure, clean and rich. I always feel that clouds come from the condensation of human breath, and that people are the streams issuing from the crevices of the earth.

Shangluo is located at the head of the ancient State of Qin and the tail end of the State of Chu. The birds above the Qinling Mountains are the plumed fish launching upwards out of the River Dan, and the fish of the River Dan are the birds from above the Qinling Mountains divested of their feathers. They are the most irrepressible creatures to be found between the heavens and the earth.

I am merely a brook trickling out of this patch of land, refracting shapes and colour. Thus my view of life surmises that men do not enter into this world to suffer. If men came here to experience tribulation, why then are there so many people on the Earth and why is it that every living person is unwilling to die? A man's life is the perfect expression of love. It originates from the lovemaking of his parents and then basks in the light of the sun, savours the irrigation of water, and imbibes the nourishment provided by food. At the same time, mankind expands and evolves. That is why everyone naturally has various musical, artistic or literary talents. It is just like the conundrum once posed by a philosopher: "When you see a flower and love it, might not the flower in fact love you more?"

Why then do conflict, hurt, jealousy and terror still afflict the world? Is it because of the competitive greed caused by overpopulation? On account of this, we assert that the dying are ferrying away a virus as they leave us. We decide that those who continue to live should be seized with gratitude towards the deceased.

I love Shangluo. I find that the mountains, waterways, vegetation, forests, birds in flight, and the scurrying animals are all dear to me. Shangluo folk are not keen to become officials. Those who set up roadside stalls and those who scrape a living by begging are decent compatriots. During these dozens of long years, whenever the sons and daughters of Shangluo have dropped by to see me in Xi'an, I have always received them with fine cigarettes, a choice selection of tea, a happy face, and a sincere heart. Never have I dared to be a poor host. When the sons and daughters of Shangluo ask me a favour, I pledge my help readily and do my utmost to prepare for the task.

Even today, my stomach still retains the memory of cracked corn porridge with sliced potatoes. My accent remains that of the southern foothills of the Qinling Mountains. Shangluo likewise cherishes me. She has permitted me to write about her for dozens of years; she has tolerated all manner of approaches. Her raw materials are rich, and her mind is broad. Whenever I have a speck of achievement, Shangluo has been the first to applaud me. If I have been frustrated, it is always Shangluo who has offered me solace.

I am but a blade of grass, a tree, a stone, a bird, a rabbit, a carrot, or a sweet potato from Shangluo. I am the seed of Shangluo, germinated in this place.

After nineteen years in Shangluo, I took up residence in Xi'an. Three times in the 1980s, I returned for tours of Shangluo venturing into almost every town and village – both large and small. In the dozens of years since then, I have still gone back and forth to Shangluo more than ten times each year. Standing at an angle to Shangluo, from the vantage point of Xi'an, I observed and ingested more about China. This is the secret of my life and the cipher for my literary career.

To date, I have set down more than ten million words. There are traces and shadows of Shangluo in all my works. In the early years, *Mountain Notes* and later the *Three Chapters About Shangzhou* and *Turbulence*, and later still *The Abandoned Capital*, *Pregnancy*, *Return to Old Gao Village*, *Missing Wolves*, as well as *Shaanxi Opera*, *Happy*, *Ancient Kiln*, *The Lantern Bearer*, and *The Mountain Whisperer* have each contributed a facet to literary Shangluo. Certain stories and anecdotes, both large and small, have had their prototype partially in Shangluo. Those who are familiar with Shangluo can detect in those works particular spots, mountains, materials, customs, characters, and dialect expressions which embody the spirit and air of the place. I cannot rid myself of Shangluo, just as I am unable to stop breathing. To put it another way, I'm like a sheep that can't shake its own scent.

A phoenix pagoda always approaches the sun,
A crane's dream always features the clouds.

I deeply appreciate Carl Jung's sentiment: "The essence of literature is to express the collective unconsciousness." Moreover, I cleave to these four words: "Robust life without ending." The most difficult and daunting task in my writing career has been to accurately grasp the collective unconsciousness of life. Still, when faced with something so primal and when attempting to capture this in writing, one cannot do it too slickly or with too much familiarity. What I feel extremely mindful about, and care deeply for, is the quest for novelty and astringency. Such a pity that I have not exactly prospered on either front.

Life really is too short. One cannot achieve manifold things. When I chose to write, other means of survival withered, so I couldn't risk being sluggish or slack. I know that I am simple and shallow in my natural constitution, and deficient in quality and talent. I'm unable to realise the utopia I've been dreaming about; unable to bring to fruition the works of my imagination. Others may be erecting an ancient Forbidden City. I am only cobbling together my country house.

A scroll hangs in my study which states: "Waiting to be under the canopy of the stars." This poses the question: when will the starlight shine on me? All I can do is set up an effigy of the Buddha and a totem of the God of the Earth (*Tudi*) in this same room. The Buddha's abilities are boundless. He can bestow favour upon all mankind, while the God of the Earth can defend my house and protect my soul.

Streams

I have grown to deeply cherish the land that nurtured me. Just as there are valleys and gullies that criss-cross the mountain, there are all manner of flowers and trees on the slopes. When I began to write about the mountains, my train of thought was aflame; my writing sprang to life.

I felt that my life and the life of my pen were the mountain streams. In these luxuriant mountains though, the waterways are pitifully thin, tender things. I always think that the rain in the sky could fall to the ground and whip up the waves of a flood, but instead when it leaves the clouds, streams strike roots which plunge into the cold land beneath the mountain. People claim that mountains are solemn; deadly silent. But this isn't true. Streams have the most intricate inner essence and possess a great vigour. Underneath the mountains, there must sit an immense sea. Its emotions are fermenting, remaining forever restless until they emerge through small brooks.

Sometimes they ooze out from a crevice, drop by drop. Or they gush, bubbling up from tiny grass roots. The sunlight is powerless to dry them into oblivion and the yellow wind cannot whip them away. Their nature is crystalline; their breath is refreshing. The moment they are born, their meandering fate is declared.

Simply because they are seeking their own path, their steps are arduous. When they slide down from the slate, they reverberate with a bewitching bronze echo. When they hurl themselves off the cliff edge, they have the hue of white silk. Swirling around in eddies and ponds, their depths become unfathomable. Gradually, they broaden and migrate further afield. They course through rocky passes, inundate grasslands, traverse bamboo groves and journey across the mountains, visiting with and enquiring about each lump of rock. Sometimes they dive abruptly beneath the sediment of riverbeds. The gentle breeze lends them a tenderness, the flowers offer them fragrance, and the bamboo donates its cool green. The excitable fish and the kaleidoscopic pebbles add exquisite charm.

They trickle on and on. Where are they going? Since it was the mountains which offered them life, I imagine they themselves should be rich and substantial. But maybe they will transform into morning dew, sprinkling themselves over buds. Or maybe they will penetrate the depths of leaves, ferrying chlorophyll for other grasses and trees. Alternatively, they could dislodge a bank of sludge or tug away a clump of rotten roots. Then, let them flow. The mountains are both vast and complex. As long as the streams surge onwards, exploring, they will pioneer their own unique paths.

The Fountain

In front of my old family home in the village, there grew an aged Chinese scholar tree which, one stormy night, was struck by lightning and split. Consequently, a letter from my family reported to me the miserable tree's tragic fate; it was snapped in two halfway up the trunk and then split into four portions. The wretched thing was fit for nothing except firewood. This message inevitably made my heart sink and I felt obliged to pay the damaged tree a special visit when next I returned to my homeland.

A vague childhood memory told me that this aged Chinese scholar tree had been standing in front of the house for ages, its great hulk withstanding the passage of time. Through scorching summers, all the neighbourhood would attach themselves to it, as it provided us with a perfect paradise for such joyful games as rope-swings, pebbles and shuttlecock. In severe winters, as the whole world fell into bleakness, the tree fought against the fierce wind with its bare arms. On such occasions, flocks of birds would perch on and warm its stark branches in return for its summer-time shade. Sometimes, the old tree conducted a lively melody. Each bird's song would echo into a lively leaf, amplifying a musical note. Upon hearing the song of winter, initiated by animated fowl, the kids rushed out of their houses, yelling gaily in the wintry outdoors.

So, I returned to my hometown after a long period of absence from the aged Chinese scholar tree. I searched with longing and in vain for its umbrella-shaped crown from the moment I approached the village entrance. It was truly gone. After stepping into the yard, my gaze immediately landed on the remains of the old tree, already chopped into a messy pile of firewood. Its glistening whiteness hurt my eyes and made my heart race. At the top of my lungs, I bellowed to my family: "How could this splendid tree vanish in an instant from the world?" Gone, together with the tree, was my sweet childhood memory of its company. Eventually, nothing was left but a bewildered, distressed stump. I could no longer be hard-hearted in the face of this cruel scene. My overwhelming tenderness towards the tree turned into tears, which trickled down my cheeks.

That night saw me sleepless. Not knowing where to wander, I sat listlessly on the stump in the yard. Since the root of the tree had not yet been dug out, the remaining stump – which was as huge as a bamboo sieve and as round as a millstone – stood solidly, glistening with a silvery light under the moon. Around the bark of the stump sprouted a ring of tiny, tender shoots, the firm length of which ranged from half an inch to a foot.

Later, my young daughter, waddling out of the house, rested her head on my lap and looked me in the eyes, sighing: "Papa, the tree is gone."

"Yes, it's gone."

"Do you miss it too?"

Her childish question awoke in me a sympathy for her. Immediately after her birth, my little girl was nursed in my hometown. Thus, the aged Chinese scholar tree had witnessed her growth from crawling infant to walking child. However, in a moment, the frolicking flash of her childhood in the company of the tree disappeared before she could savour it.

"Papa," my little daughter blurted out. "I can hear leaves whispering like murmuring water."

Oh, my funny girl, why did you speak such sentimental words, calling up long held memories of a watery tune? Now I knew the pity that this water melody would never be heard again.

"Papa, the water is still there!" my daughter marvelled. "Look, isn't the stump exactly like a fountain?" As I turned around, the sight of the stump now astonished me. It was a fountain! Under the moonbeam, the snow-white woodiness became the water-shadow, while the growth rings were ripples moving out from the water source. My heart was filled with gratitude for my adorable daughter who had discovered this. In my eyes, she was as great as Christopher Columbus.

Bubbling over with enthusiasm, I held my daughter close to my chest and exclaimed: "This fountain is a fountain of life." It is true that the facts of the world are more diverse than the fictions of the mind (this fabulous world always surprises with its unpredictability). But in this instance, I knew that a tree is an upright river, the streams of which could be easily blocked by a thunderbolt. Its spring may gush out an inexhaustible supply of fresh water. Each of the extending, criss-crossing roots running deep underground is a spring of the headwaters.

On this moonlit night, I gazed at the shoots proliferating from the bark of the stump. Each leaf was bursting into bright verdure. My mind began to run wild: these green crystals, these angels, are they not pillars of water spilling from the fountain? Are the dewdrops on the sawtoothed leaves not foam left behind by the splashing water? Alas, within every bit of foam there is a little moon, which sheds shiny flickers of splendour at night.

"Papa, could the tender branches eventually grow up?"
"You bet," I answered.

Afterwards, the quiet night saw us sitting wordless beside the fountain. We were listening attentively to the splashing water of life in the air.

My Primary School

My primary school was housed in a temple; the building was very tall, with carved flying dragons and running beasts along the beams. The crevices between the tiles were grouted with green moss all year-round. On rainy days, a fleshy kind of weed called groundsel shot out from the surrounding earth and seemed to grow six inches in height. The teachers lodged in the temple lofts. In former times, there had been a statue of Guanyu enshrined there, his face as red as a date. Later people moved him away and constructed a courtyard on the muddy foundations. The eyes of the deity were made of glazed porcelain beads, but after the school stood it on top of the screen wall at the entrance, its corneas could only emanate a faint light in the darkening dusk.

The rooms on either side of the courtyard served as classrooms; only students in the senior grades took lessons there. The steps to the temple were extremely steep. I could jump down them with both feet, but could only scale them one at a time. I often preferred to make a detour around the corner of the wall. From there, I would happily hop along the stone-paved path on one foot. At the corner of the wall was an ancient chinaberry tree with a cracked trunk. A crow's nest as large as a bamboo sieve was balanced in the canopy. Underneath it hung a bell which, whenever it was struck, never appeared to ruffle the family of birds. For a few years, I wracked my brain over this queer phenomenon.

At the age of five, my mother hauled me over to the temple to enrol. The school refused me at first, so I fastened myself to the leg of the office table and wailed. The teachers laughed and then relented but I was still not officially registered as pupil. Instead, they admitted me as a "probationer" in the reception class. My mother insisted that I should kowtow to the teachers and so I knelt obediently, my head making a thudding sound as it struck the floor. A teacher scooped me up and I was worried that she might be about to tug at my ears. Her plump, meaty hand pinched away some nasal snivel. "You are a student now. How can you still have the runny nose of a toddler?" Everyone guffawed at my lost dignity. I was shamefaced. From then on, being afraid that mucus could once again drip from my nose, but owning no handkerchief, I carried a pocketful of poplar leaves. On entering the building, I would spruce myself up.

As there were few classrooms and we were only the reception grade, there were no seats for us in the temple courtyard. We had to be taught in the Liu Family Memorial Hall outside the religious house. A blackboard was suspended there for us, and earthen bricks were stacked up to support a tabletop. When the riverbed dried up in the summer, the villagers tore the planks away from the bridge to serve as desks. We each had to bring our own stool. At that time, my extended family had not yet been divided into new households by marriage, and having so many older paternal cousins but not enough seats to go around, I often went without. What is more, owing to my height, it was always hard for me to reach the desk and I was forced to stand up during lessons. If my legs became numb, I would scavenge a wooden slat from home and drive both ends into the stacks on which the table-top was balanced. The batten duly served as my seat. Uncomfortable as it was, at least I never dozed off. My only regret was that after class I couldn't join in the others' games. They turned their stools upside down and slid themselves along the slope behind the hall playing "cars". I could only squat and ride around on my backside. I would lose my balance and somersault earthwards with a face full of dust.

As there was no clock at home, we could not keep time in the morning and so I was often late. After much crying and nagging, my mother decided to rise earlier, spending her hours stitching shoe soles under the light of a lamp while waiting for the peal of the school bell. In winter, when we got up, the moonlight was still strong, and we would yell out for our classmates in the surrounding houses, accompanying each other to school. Everyone had a satchel apart from me. My mother gave me a square of cloth to bundle my things tightly together and tuck under my arm. At that time, I was very eager to outdo others, and fell short in every respect. Mother told me that this couldn't be helped because we had no money to spare. When we arrived, the door of the hall was locked and the school monitor, who wasn't there yet, had the key. We would begin to dance a jig we had learnt called "Looking for Friends": "Look for, look for, look for a good friend! At last we've found one!" Everyone was very merry. Sometimes I took Xiaoni as my pal in the jig and sometimes Fangfang.

By the time we reached the Third Grade, we had stopped this kind of horseplay and boys and girls would sit apart. Once, I played dropkick the shuttlecock with Fangfang and my classmates teased me and referred to us as "husband and wife". They would tap an accusing finger against their cheek and from that moment we became estranged. When the monitor came, we would file in and assume our seats. It was pitch-dark inside. Sometimes we would burn pine tar for a light source, but most of the time we fumbled to our seats in the blackness. There were friezes painted on the walls of the memorial hall. I can remember the legend of the dutiful Wang Xiang using his body heat to melt the frozen lake, to catch fish for his stepmother. Not being able to understand the underlying meaning – that of filial sacrifice – the image of his body on the lake filled us with fear. Nobody dared lean their chairs against the walls, or mention the contents of the frescoes. We just closed our eyes and began to recite the text from lesson one. As soon as one student fell silent, the rest followed suit and a hush descended on the hall. The wind rattled away at the hemp paper covering the window lattice, making everyone fearful. All at once, the recitations resumed, our voices becoming ever louder in an effort to fortify ourselves. Otherwise, if one was to flee, the rest would follow and I would certainly be the last straggler, screaming and caterwauling in unearthly tones.

Facing the platform in the memorial hall was a lily pond. In the winter, as the leaves withered and the water froze, we would forage for bird's eggs among the reeds. Or we might snap off the dried stalks of the lilies and set them alight, the smoke collecting in plumes. Often this brought out the mucus from our noses, and we'd choke as tears filled our eyes.

We sat in this memorial hall for two years. Our teacher was the lady who had wiped my nose. She had a preternaturally white complexion and spoke sweetly to the class. She would read a text aloud as though singing. I had never heard such an alluring voice. For the first half of my school years, I barely understood what she was saying yet, in every lesson, I found myself intoxicated by the strains of her melody. Whenever she asked me to rise and answer a question, I was totally lost for words. Then she would say: "You really are a probationer, through and through."

Until then, none of my classmates knew my true status, so after she divulged the secret, everyone looked down on me. In all the exercises we did after this, they would extend a little finger, dip it in their saliva, and sing: "Hmm, what can a probationer do?" I fought with them many times, but my mother punished me with a clouting and denied me dinner. When my teacher heard about this, she apologised to my mother and me. She admitted her blame in the matter, and asked if I had trouble understanding her class. I answered: "I only take in the sound of your voice. It's so sweet." Blushing, she smiled. From then on, I resolved never to let myself fall behind the others. My teacher also treated me more attentively. Her voice was still mellifluous. After class she would tutor me – something which filled everyone else with envy.

After the first grade, my teacher told me: "You are still too young. We cannot let you advance to the class above." I felt scared and burst into tears. My teacher gathered me in her arms, confessed to jesting, and declared me no longer a probationer. So great was my relief that I instinctively called her "auntie". I was struck with embarrassment. She didn't seem annoyed and simply pinched me on the mouth. She smiled and so did I. In the afternoon she came to my house with my class score. In front of my mother, she praised me and remarked on my good behaviour and rapid progress. My mother poached an egg for her. Emboldened, I declared: "Your voice is so lovely. Can you sing a song for me?" As she began to trill, two deep dimples appeared on her cheeks and afterwards she giggled.

When summertime came, we were given a lunchtime siesta. We were terribly mischievous. While others rested, bent over their desks, some of us would slip out to the lily pond. The bravest would wade in at the deep end, then doggy paddle, tread water or do the backstroke with their tiny bellies poking above the surface. Timid as I was, I would grip the roots of the tree by the edge and whip up waves with my feet. The girls always snitched, so we were inspected for the telltale blanching that comes from a long dip. Inevitably, we were scolded. The water was seductive though and we couldn't tear ourselves away from it. Soon we started waving our fists at the girls. We would hide our clothes among the bushes and head straight for the deep end. Once, the headmaster discovered us there and upbraided our poor teacher to the point of tears. After hearing what had happened, we confessed our crime to the teacher and began to revile the head. We dug a pit before the entrance to the memorial hall and used it to bury a chubby clay effigy of him. Again, the girls told on us. Our teacher asked several of us to stand up in front of the class and meted out a tongue lashing. Later, when she knew I was the ringleader, she pushed me out of the classroom so fiercely that I lost one of the buttons from my coat. When class was over, she sewed it back on, but my face was now soaked by tears. Overnight, I wrote an essay of self-criticism, then left it on display in the classroom for three whole days.

At that time, I loved Chinese Language lessons most of all, and especially enjoyed composing sentences. Each one I wrote was excessively long, so I got through plenty of exercise books. Later, I frequented the graveyard at Yellow Slope and pilfered the white paper mourners left behind. At home, I bound them into long, narrow notebooks. When Tomb-Sweeping Day came around, I could bind ten volumes in a single day. Nonetheless, when I was composing my mammoth sentences, there were many characters I couldn't visualise, so I had to spell them phonetically or use homonyms. My classmates all called me the "Monarch of Misspelling", though the teacher always praised me for having a nimble brain. Every time my homework would be graded "excellent", but she would underline the incorrect words in red and ask me to copy them out in their proper form three times. Learning calligraphy was also a favourite, even though I didn't own a brush. Once, I tried to snip some wool from my uncle's lambskin mattress and fashion a brush. When my teacher offered me a brush of my own, my heart was filled with gratitude and I became even fonder of the discipline. Where others would turn out one practice piece, I would produce two or three. The teacher would pin these up on the classroom wall and, later, display them in the senior students' classroom. She took me over for a visit. As the teacher's desk was so high, it eclipsed me. She picked me up and planted my feet on a chair to see my work. I continued to use that brush until it was bald, and even then, could not bring myself to throw it away. I hid it inside a Song Dynasty vase at home. During the Cultural Revolution, when the "Four Olds" were being smashed, that piece of china was confiscated with the brush inside.

During my time in the first and second grades, my father worked away from home. Whenever my mother wanted to write a letter to him, she would take a few eggs to the teacher and beg her to act as the scribe. She consented, but refused the gift. In the latter half of the second grade, my teacher asked me: "Now that you can compose sentences yourself, why don't you try writing to your father?" I told her that I didn't understand the letter format. She said: "Only your family is meant to see it, so you don't need to be a stickler for the rules." I really made the effort. Since I knew all the goings-on in my family, I wanted to relate them to him. I wanted him to know that my grandma was recovering from her illness and no longer hacked away at night.

My mother was in the pink, though she kept on nagging about the weather and she worried my father might not be wearing his cotton-padded clothing. Our pet rabbit had given birth to six babies. Our dog continued to be ferocious; it had bitten Sanwa's leg. The truth was that it was acting in retaliation from first being struck with a stick. I wanted my father to know that I had fared well in the school examinations, scoring 100% in Arithmetic and 98% in Chinese Language. I wanted him to know that I was penalised for writing one incorrect character.

In the end, it took me three whole days to complete the letter. My teacher corrected many spelling mistakes, but she said: "In future, when you advance to the higher grades, or when you're grown up and want to write a long article, just write in this fashion. Don't be bound by any of the set formats. Write whatever you want to write about whatever you're familiar with, as long as you can make your words concrete and clear." From then on, I have held my teacher's words in my mind. Nowadays, I believe it is down to her influence that I can turn my hand to both fiction and essay writing.

That year, we completed the second grade. We were elated because, as third grade students, we were permitted to board inside the temple. During the winter vacation, we all foraged for herbs and chopped wood for pocket money. We discussed buying New Year pictures for our teacher at Spring Festival. On the morning of New Year's Eve (according to the lunar calendar), we assembled with the paintings and some firecrackers with the intention of visiting her. She was nowhere to be found. Our headmaster reported that she had been transferred. He took out a parcel of sweets and informed us that when our teacher was preparing to leaving, she had really wanted to visit the home of each of her students. Time was limited though, so she left behind the confectionery to be distributed among us when the new term began. We all broke down in tears. I never caught sight of my teacher again. I studied in the temple for a further four years and then in a secondary school fifteen *li* away for another three years. I never found out the whereabouts of my first teacher. Now, twenty-five years have passed and I have no idea whether she is still in this world or not. Whenever I recall this story, I come over low-spirited.

Stories from Dihua

Dihua is a township in Shangluo consisting of sixteen hamlets.

I.

Bai Liang, from the settlement at Bai Family Strip, was eating supper as he sat outside under the eaves of the courtyard. With his head bowed, searching for the beans in his bowl, he heard a slapping sound – a fish had appeared on the floor. The fish was tossing itself around. Bai Liang thought maybe someone had caught it in the nearby river and thrown it over for him. Out loud, he asked: "Who is it?" No answer was forthcoming, so he peered around. All he could see was a man with his back turned at the entrance of the lane, but in the poor light of the setting sun he could not make out who it was. The man's feet seemed ungrounded somehow, as if floating on the surface of water. Or else some hidden force appeared to be causing him to levitate. After passing the willow tree at the entrance to the lane, the man simply vanished.

Bai Liang wondered if this was San Hai. He had helped San Hai to build the walls of his courtyard, and he had been flushed with gratitude for this favour. Was it he who had gifted the fish? But San Hai had been sick and bedridden for more than a month. How could he go out angling? Could it have been Bai Lu's second son, Shuipi? Shuipi spent the whole day, every day, fishing. Once he had caught a fish, he would take it to the highway and sell it to a passing motorist. Why would he send one to Bai Liang for no apparent reason?

Bai Liang returned to the courtyard to inspect the fish. He found it totally without scales. A tiny cloud hovered over its smooth body. He realised the fish had fallen from the heavens.

People think of the Milky Way as a silver river. Could there be fish in its waters? Or might a crane have picked up a fish from the stream in Dihua and carelessly let it slip from its bill while flying over the courtyard?

Bai Liang felt the fish was a good omen. He gazed at the sky for a long time, wondering if a pie might follow the fish. No pie came, just a gust of wind. The breeze blew over a poplar leaf which had drifted onto Bai Liang's face. He picked up the fish and took it inside to braise.

The next day, he carried his shoulder pole to the river to collect water. A fish and a cat were tussling away in the shallows by the bank. Maybe the fish had swum to the edge and the cat had lunged down to bite it? The tail of the fish beat ripples in the water, and several times the moggy pitched backwards, getting its posterior wet. Bai Liang put down his buckets and went to drive the cat away. Remarkably, he discovered that the fish had fur and wings. As he was pondering this, the fish launched into the depths and disappeared.

How could a fish have fur and wings?

Bai Liang saw something else about a hundred metres upriver. As the fish darted away, an entire shoal leapt from the water and flew into the air, while – simultaneously – a flock of birds dived into the river one by one. Birds plunged downwards and fish shot upwards. The cycle repeated itself. One moment they were fish, the next they were birds.

From then on, Bai Liang's behaviour and manner became increasingly eccentric. For example, when he quarrelled with his neighbour about the boundary line between their properties, the other fellow cursed him, calling him a "grass-reared ruminant". Bai Liang agreed. When the villagers heard, they couldn't understand how he could allow himself to be maligned in this way. He replied that he had in fact been raised on a diet of grass. Were vegetables not a kind of grass? Were rice and wheat flour not made from grass seed? His gait also changed. His arms now swung back and forth gaily, as if he was wildly doggy-paddling in the river. People laughed at him, but he responded: "Do you think that air is not water?"

II.

Wu Fu, from Jiayuan Village, had been practising *qigong* for three years and gained quite a reputation for it. He invited some women to stand with their eyes closed while he transmitted his telekinetic power from five paces away. He asked them: "Can you feel the lick of the cold wind?" The women replied: "Yeah, yeah, it's come over all chilly!"

When people in Dihua knew that Wu Fu had mastered *qigong*, they begged him to cure their diseases. Wu Fu refused to treat headaches and fever. Those could be easily remedied with a bowl of ginger soup and by sweating it out under heavy quilts. Instead, he devoted his energies to defeating cancer. In Dihua, many residents were afflicted. Poor as they were, most could not afford to go to the provincial hospital for surgery. He charged no fee for his services, merely pronouncing: "Spreading the news of what I'm able to do is reward enough."

Wu Fu was very particular about finding the correct

location to treat his patients. Usually, he would operate at the foot of the cliff behind the village. A cypress tree of more than a century old grew down there and he liked to clamber up it and gather the *qi* it gave off. He would then ask the patient to sit down as he stretched out his arms, palms facing towards them. This channelled the *qi* in their direction. On 14th July 1998, while he was doing this, a gust of wind struck up, intensifying to gale force. He was whipped from his feet and propelled violently against the cliff face. When things died down, he came loose and plopped down to the earth like a meat patty.

III.

The Erlang Temple can be found on Eastern Street. In front of it is the Scholar Deity's Tower. The two buildings are separated by a sprawling square. Local people used to call it "the temple playground". Shuan Lao made his home here. He was ugly and penniless, but owned one decent sheet. All through the summer he refrained from sleeping indoors because he loathed the stultifying heat and the marauding mosquitoes. Dusk would find him heading for the playground with his thin blanket. After clearing a patch of ground, he would bed down draped with the sheet. The next morning he would be spotted climbing down from the nearby tower. The Scholar Deity's Tower was extremely tall, and you could only reach as far as the third storey by using gaps in the external brickwork as footholds. The wind merrily caressed the top of the steeple. The villagers decided that Shuan Lao must have performed a miracle, flying up to the tower around midnight. When people asked him about the matter, he simply smiled. He would neither admit nor deny the rumour.

Later, Shuan Lao went to Xi'an to make a living, taking his sheet with him. He was gone for three years. Somehow the villagers continued to gossip about him. They said he was making a living as a thief. They said that the sheet gave him the power to leap onto roofs and vault over walls.

In 2002, when SARS was rife, the sixteen hamlets of Dihua organised a crisis team to patrol and be prepared to fight intruders. People from Xi'an were prohibited from entering the village. It was right around this time that Shuan Lao came back. The team chased after him as a makeshift battalion and he was driven as far as the cliff on the western side of Dihua. The river ran below the precipice. Someone shouted that they should stop their pursuit, fearful he would be toppled into the water below. Someone else reminded the crowd that it didn't matter: his sheet gave him the power of flight from the savage current. As the mob assailed him with sticks and clubs, Shuan Lao jumped from the cliff.

Whether the fall left him dead or alive, it is only known that he did not return and no news was ever heard about him.

In the winter, a profusion of bats appeared on the cliff face. One villager suggested that they were the reincarnation of Shuan Lao. When the bats spread their wings, it looked like they were carrying a tiny sheet. At once, another voice objected to their foolishness – the bat sheets were black, not white.

IV.

Shang Cao, from Gong Family Village, had a flash of inspiration while pumping up his bike tyre. He felt compelled to practice one *kung fu* move everyday – grasping a handful of air and then flinging it like an invisible projectile at the dog. The dog did not react. One day when he was practicing, he heard someone calling for him from the entrance to the lane: "Shang Cao! Shang Cao!" The tone was urgent. He raised his head to find that a plume of grey smoke was billowing in his direction. When it reached his feet, it dawned on him that this was a dog. Another wisp of smoke had already reached the top of his head. He grasped for a broom from within the haze and struck out. Unexpectedly, a pigeon dropped down. The bird flapped its wings on the ground for a while before flying away. Then two more twists of smoke appeared, inching towards him. He thought: "What could they be?" On peering hard at them, it became clear that his Pa and Ma were approaching him. Both had a basket of sweet potatoes strapped to their backs. He realised his mouth had dropped open, but he was too startled to make a sound.

His Ma said: "I called you eight or ten times, but not a peep. I wanted you to go to the field and fetch sweet potatoes."

Shang Cao stared at his parents and swished his hand before his face. His Pa and Ma were not smoke that could be batted away.

His Pa asked: "What's the matter?"

"My eyes are foggy."

"You're so young. How could this happen?"

He went to lay down the broom. As he did so, it became soft and slipped through his fingers. A plume of smoke. The gathering fog became more intense by the road that ran along the entrance to the lane. The sound of people bustling about could be heard from within the pall. You may as well be blind, for all the good having sight does for you in the darkness of evening. When he sat by his front door, he could tell who was coming by the particular noise their footsteps made on the path. He worked out that the folks who were talking were his second great uncle, Laixi's father, his wife, Chun Cao, and Auntie Chan. Even though their voices were audible, the people themselves were invisible. Every last one of them had become a column of smoke, whether thick or thin. They took the shape of either a cotton cloud or a wispy strip.

Shang Cao followed the columns of smoke. Sometimes they reassumed the shape of a human, then reverted to smoke again.

Shang Cao walked from the entrance of the lane to the road beyond. He continued until he reached the field by the riverbank, a basket of sweet potatoes on his back. As he was making his way home, he abruptly lost his bearings. There was no village in the direction from which he had come. The newly built houses, the trees and the earthen path had all disappeared, leaving nothing behind except smoke. He stood there for a long time. The smoke rose up like a mushroom, seething and somersaulting. In an instant, it came crashing to the ground. Gradually, another metamorphosis occurred; the smoke was transformed back into houses, trees and straight earthen paths. Grasshoppers were bounding about.

Shang Cao told the villagers what he had experienced. Everyone agreed that there must have been something wrong with his eyes. Shang Cao then felt certain that there was a problem with his vision. Within half a year, he had become totally blind.

V.

Elm Liu, son of the Liu Family from Middle Street Village, had an unlucky name. Elm trees grow disobediently. For over thirty years, Elm Liu refused to obey his Pa. When the sun came out and he was asked to hang out the quilt, he would build a chicken coop instead. When his Pa told him to sow peppers, he would plant potatoes.

On reaching the age of fifty-six, his Pa became afflicted with ascites in his belly and was seized by the desire to build his tomb on Cow Head Slope behind the village. After all, that was where all the villagers were interred. However, he was afraid of spending too much, so he insisted: "Don't waste money." Applying some reverse psychology on his errant son, he added: "Just bury me on our own land by the riverbank." For decades, Elm Liu refused to listen to his Pa, but in this solemn instance, he thought he would comply. When his Pa died, he followed his instructions to the letter and buried his father on their land by the riverbank. The third year after the funeral, a flood demolished the bank and swept the grave clean away.

Originally, the river was the habitat for a kind of fish known as the "sawbelly". After the flood, a new type appeared, known as the "rasping catfish". It was so named because of the noise it made. The creature seemed to be always sighing in regret.

VI.

Kuanxin was a workshy fellow born in the village of Wild Cat Hollow. He remained a lifelong bachelor. When he died, his eyes closed but his mouth remained agape. The neighbours who came over to tend to him discovered a stream of white breath emanating from his lips and drifting out through the window. They ran outside to find that the mist did not dissipate. Rather, it floated up to the top of the toon tree and morphed into a cloud as big as a fan before hovering away to the west.

As if absorbed in meditation, the cloud paused the moment it reached Western Street Village. The sunlight cast its shadow onto the roof of Old Tian's house, but then the cloud hurried on. Later, it traversed the whole of Tableland Slack, Gong Family Bend, and finally stopped in motionless suspension above Flint Ge's courtyard in Foot-of-the-Cliff Village.

Flint Ge kept a boar for impregnating all the sows of Dihua. That day, it happened that Starry Lu was dragging a female pig from Camel Hump Village to be cross-bred with the boar. The shadow of the cloud fell in line with the sow's body, turning it from white to black. Starry Lu looked up at the sky. A shred of cloud dropped down like a handkerchief. Instinctively, he recoiled from as if it were about to knock him unconscious. Relieved that this was not to be, he carried on his journey.

Usually the sow would deliver an entire litter of piglets, but this time only one arrived. The baby appeared sweet, though didn't grow as it should have done. Half a year past and it remained tiny and slender, always wanting to jostle playfully around with the cat. Starry Lu said: "You're a piggy, aren't you? Why don't you get bigger?" The swine still showed no sign of maturing. By the end of the year, it weighed only forty or fifty pounds. Strange red bristles covered its entire body.

The following spring, swine fever swept through Dihua, claiming the lives of eight pigs, including the little runt. When it was breathing its last, Starry Lu noticed a stream of white breath emanating from its maw and floating skywards, where it consolidated into a cloud. This time, the cloud was no larger than a man's palm.

As the cloud travelled over North Canal Village, a breeze whipped up, pushing it towards the south and Wild Cat Hollow. In the reed beds of the hollow, wadding was wafting about, becoming indistinguishable from the cloud. When a bee landed on one of the lilac buds, the fluffy matter became caught in the branches of a tree and the cloud disappeared. When the lilac withered and broke into seed, the seeds trickled into the crevices of the earth. The next year, a lilac sapling sprang up. In its second year it was still no taller. The grazing cattle tugged it out at the root and proceeded to chew. As soon as the lilac was uprooted, a stream of white breath emanated from the earth. This time it clumped into a coin-sized gasp. Gliding over the courtyard wall, it reached the mosquito-infested dykes. One more mosquito materialised.

On finding its wings, this mosquito sped over to the threshing ground. There the ranks of the sweltering were slumbering and relishing the cool of evening. The insect set about nipping them on the legs and, with a swat of a palm, wound up squashed. No cloud appeared; not even a wisp of white breath.

VII.

Lei Family Slope was home to no one of that name. There

were two sizeable clans – one named Yu and the other Tian. The Tians were all stumpy-legged and thick-necked. The Yus towered in height and wore pinched faces. Men outnumbered women in the former family and vice versa in the latter, giving the Tians the whip hand in the village.

There is a coal mine in Luonan County, fifty *li* to the north of Dihua. In the early years of the colliery, a man from the Tian clan went there to dig and progressed to the role of contractor of the pits. As his earnings multiplied, he became a well-to-do boss. He brought his male relatives over to join him in the work, allowing everyone a stake in the operation. The Yu family continued to be downtrodden, so the womenfolk headed to Dihua to train as home helps. After assessment and tutorage, eight of them were selected by the domestic agency in Xi'an. They were happily assigned to the households of senior cadres.

The next spring, the coal miners returned with full pockets. Before they reached their village, the team spent a night in a hotel in the county town. The gossips among the Yu family insisted that the miners were gorging on meat and knocking back liquor, even soliciting the services of call-girls. It was rumoured that the sex workers spouted black piss for three days.

After the festivities of New Year, the men of the Tian family resumed their digging. On 24th of January, according to the lunar calendar, a firedamp explosion tore through the pit, leaving no survivors. It was on that same day that the home helps returned to the village. They entertained the villagers with tales of being flown to Beijing and Guangzhou with their employers. They described their surprise at the toilets on the plane; sucking all the crap and piss downwards and out into the air.

On 8th April every year, the people of Dihua would stage a traditional New Year carnival with masks and acrobatics. Middle Street Village prepared two main floats. One displayed a hell of devils and running beasts; the other, a paradise of birds in flight. During rehearsals, some worried that the central theme might prove an ill omen – a harbinger of trouble for Lei Family Slope – so the event was cancelled.

VIII.

Cashew Tree Village was in north-west Dihua. Apart from the gargantuan cashew tree, the village slope was swathed with date trees. Each year, a few of the date trees was felled by lightning. These lightning-spliced dates conceived a kind of soul. The *yin-yang* master from the county town came to search for such timber to fashion into instruments of divination. When the villagers went out, they would all carry a small wooden token hewn from the date wood in their pockets. It was purported that these could safeguard their owners by driving away any approaching malevolence.

One summer day three years ago, Youliang was grazing his cow on the hillside. A peal of thunder echoed across the sky, so he drove his cow down the slope. This time lightning targeted Youliang. He was lucky, but a set of hieroglyphs erupted on the skin of his back. Perhaps they were Chinese characters, but the teachers in Dihua primary school were at a loss as to how to read them. The eighteen signs were divided into three rows. Though they were a sore shade of red, as though scratched by fingernails, they were neither itchy nor painful.

By the end of autumn, Youliang had been struck down

by a creeping paralysis. Also, his hands and feet shrank, leaving him quite helpless. He could not feed himself or walk unaided. All he could do was sit in his bamboo chair at home being waited on by others. Even so, Youliang now had the gift to predict the approach of the wind and rain. One day, the sun shone crimson but he maintained that there would be hailstones. Nobody believed him. Before his neighbours had time to finish a pipeful of tobacco, balls of ice were hurtling down with a *pah-pi-pah-pah*.

Once in the middle of the night, Youliang woke his family and told them that stones were about to fall from the sky and to hurry out into the courtyard. They trusted his prediction, sitting outdoors until daybreak. Still, no stones came. As they were about to head inside, a blaze flashed overhead and something thudded against the roof with a *pu-tong*. On inspection, and as foretold, a large stone shard lay in a crater nearby, having torn through the roof.

IX.

Thirteenth Brother Han in West Street Village was a dreamer. The second he nodded off, he began to dream. When he awoke, he had crystal clear memories of the dream. At the age of three, he dreamed about turning into an old man with a shaggy white beard. Wielding a wooden sword, this dreamy chap climbed a high wall to perform a jig. On hearing his account, others snorted: "A likely story! How could you perform a sword dance and balance on high?" Nonetheless, people found it humorous that he could dream every day and also have perfect recall. Whenever they ran into him, they would ask: "Little fella, what did you dream of this time?" Thirteenth Brother Han replied that he had seen himself walking in a place where the road was long and broad. On either side of the road were houses of colossal stature. Each storey was engineered from glass, and the traffic below gushed more densely than a river torrent. A man in white was gesturing with his hands and feet like a warlock. A few of the villagers who had been to Xi'an imagined that this must be the city and so enquired: "Okay, that's one street, but what else can you find there?" He explained that trees lined the roadside and every one of them was spangled with stars.

As he grew older, Thirteenth Brother Han's dreams became increasingly esoteric. And yet they all pertained in some way to elements found in Xi'an. In primary school, he had dreamed about manning a wok in a restaurant with a chef's hat on his head. It wasn't sliced potatoes or beansprouts that he was tossing about in the oil. For whatever reason, he was frying peculiar, almost alien kinds of fish and shrimps. In high school, his slumbering mind was captivated with the image of a mighty hammer, a saw and a brush. He was slathering paint against somebody's wall. The lady of the house kindly sent him a uniform, but cursed him on another occasion.

Such dreams persisted for three years. Since he failed the university entrance exam, he was forced to labour in the village. He served as the community accountant. He fired bricks and tiles before getting married and having children. His dreams continued. One day, during his slumbers, he found himself in the city, and realised that the wall he had danced atop before was the same one that encircles the city. From the vantage point of this fortification, he could see the shining gilded roof of the bell tower. Around that time, several villagers made the journey to Xi'an seeking odd jobs. He asked them: "Is there a bell tower in Xi'an?" The answer was affirmative. He then asked: "Can people drive vehicles on top of the wall?" Again, they replied "yes". Thirteenth Brother Han decided he should follow them to the city.

In Xi'an, he found that every detail of his dreams tallied with reality. He felt a familiarity with the cityscape. He found himself in the same restaurant where he had seen himself employed as a cook. Two stone lions flanked the entrance to that establishment. The eyes of the one on the right were painted red. Unfortunately, his lack of skills and capital meant he was reduced to collecting street trash. The first day on the job, he was over the moon to pocket thirty yuan. He calculated that if he repeated this, in ten days he would earn three hundred yuan and in one month, nine hundred. So, the next morning, he woke early and walked out the door to work. He was promptly mown down by a haulage truck. The driver bolted and it was a full hour before Thirteenth Brother Han was discovered and sent to the hospital. He was DOA.

That year he had turned thirty.

An epitaph was set up in front of his tomb, on which was chiselled: "Born 1978; Died 2000." After some time had passed, the inscription read differently: "Born 1980; Died 2040." The villagers could not fathom how it was that the numbers had been altered.

x.

Dihua township government office was constructed in Middle Street Village. It was made up of a new courtyard with high walls and a newly wrought iron gate. The doorman there was still the old-timer of the surname Ye. No one had ever addressed him as "Old Ye" because that sounded like an expression for "Old Pa". Rather, they called him "Old Swarthy".

Old Swarthy had been serving as doorman since 1958. At that time, the township was known as a "commune". Old Swarthy was now eighty years old. His eyes no longer bloomed and his ears had turned stone deaf. Nonetheless, he was still in relatively fair fettle and the township kept him on to mind the entrance. The truth is that the natives of Dihua are seldom long-lived.

Almost everyone has their regrets. There are those who spend decades worried and vexed about the business of raising and marrying off their children. Others tear down their old homes and erect new ones. But now that the people had plenty to eat and drink, they had nothing of which to be afraid. They would say: "All is right as rain. Now is the time to enjoy life." Nonetheless, within two years, or at most five, whoever had spoken these words would drop dead, in an endless morbid pattern.

On the other hand, Old Swarthy was a high-spirited octogenarian. Many sought after the secret of his longevity. He would respond that as soon as he had finished pressing dumplings on New Year's Eve, he would resume setting out the plan for his future life. To date, he had plotted out what to do until the age of 120. He would list in detail what must be accomplished each year and precisely how he would tackle it. Pharmacist Wang, from the Chinese apothecary on the street, once caught sight of the plan for his centenary year. Wang told the others that Old Swarthy's great-grandson was scheduled to be married this particular May. The nuptials required a new residence, so Old Swarthy would need to cough up three thousand yuan. What is more, he would be dredging the well in the courtyard and installing an electric-powered pump. The other business jotted down for that year was in relation to the township government elections. A new Head would come into office – the forty-fifth under whom he would have served. When all was told, he would endeavour to see off seventy of them.

Beyond the western wall of the township courtyard, there grew an ancient Manchurian catalpa tree. It didn't belong to the government; it was the property of Liu Fanzheng. No tree in Dihua was more statuesque than this. At dusk, folk from Middle Street Village would assemble to talk beneath its shade. They would discuss how long it had lived, then segue naturally into how long Old Swarthy had been alive. One fellow, named Kuanxi, decided to follow his example and began to sketch out his life plan until the age of 100.

Kuanxi passed at the age of sixty-two.

Another man from Middle Street Village by the name of Bull Rope had endured a long, difficult life. He wanted desperately to know when he would die and asserted that when he died his troubles would end. He visited Old Swarthy and asked: "Kuanxi was determined to live to a great age, so how come he kicked the bucket? Does this mean that your plan is total humbug?" Old Swarthy said: "Kuanxi was a cadre from the county government. He retired and had nothing to do. How could the God of Hell allow such an idler to hang around in this world? People make plans when they have countless things to do. You don't live for the sake of being alive. Kuanxi wanted to carry on but he couldn't. By contrast, you want to die but you can't! You're sandwiched between youth and old age. How can you die without fulfilling what needs to be done?"

One night, six months after their conversation, Old Swarthy was sitting by the gate. He heard the rustling of the catalpa tree, which sounded like a sigh, then: "Oh, ah. Leaving. I'm leaving."

The next day Liu Fanzheng suffered a fatal brain haemorrhage. His son felled the tree for a coffin.

From that moment on, the tree was missed at the entrance of the township government courtyard. Old Swarthy stayed put all the same. The newly-appointed Head had been in his post for only seven days, and every evening so far, the doorman would narrate to him some vignette from the history of Dihua.

A Very Ugly Stone

I'll always feel regret about the ugly stone that used to lie by our house. Its dark expanse had the air of a sprawling bovine. Nobody knew when it was left there and nobody took much notice of it. Only when the wheat was being cut and our harvest spread before our house to dry did Grandma say: "That rock's so unsightly; it's a waste of space. Find some time and lug it away."

When my uncle was building a house nearby, he thought to install it as a gable. He abandoned that plan owing to the rock's bizarre shape – with no sharp edges or smooth planes. People were reluctant to try and lift a chisel to it; they didn't think it worth the energy. The river strand was not far away and any random rock taken from there would prove superior to this one. As soon as my uncle's house was finished, he deemed the rock unsuitable for serving as a doorstep. One year, a stonemason visited us, hoping to carve us a grindstone. My grandma said: "Use this beastly lump. No need to haul something from afar." The mason inspected it and shook his head, complaining that the texture was too fine and not at all workable. It was not delicate like the white marble of the Han Dynasty, which could be incised with characters or blossoms. Nor was it smooth like dolerite, which lent itself to both washing silk and pounding laundry. It just lay quietly prostrate, unable to enjoy the fullness of the shade offered by the Chinese scholar tree that stood close by. No flowers bloomed at the rock's edges, only sods of creeping wild grass. Gradually, it became encrusted with moss and tarnished with dark spots. Even the kids in the neighbourhood despised it and once tried to rally everyone to tug it away. Even our collective strength was no match for the stubborn rock. From time to time, we would spew vile curses at it, venting our intense dislike. Nonetheless, we were entirely impotent and had to leave it undisturbed.

What gave us a shred of consolation was the knowledge that it bore a not insubstantial hole. On rainy days, this would fill with water. It was often the case that when the rains had stopped for three days and the land lay dry, there was still water in this pit. Chickens might peck refreshment from it. On the fifteenth day of every month, we expected the full moon to rise. Then we would climb onto the rock and gaze at the distant horizon. Grandma would always scold us for fear we might tumble off. One time, I did just that and my knee was left badly grazed. Everyone continued to curse it as an ugly stone. That it was – hideous beyond reason.

After a time, an astronomer came to the village. Passing by our home, he caught sight of the stone. He straightened up and locked eyes on it. He then chose to settle in the community. Later, other astronomers came at his bidding and judged that it was a fragment of meteorite that had fallen to earth two or three centuries ago. It was therefore an artefact of considerable value. Soon after that, a truck pulled up and it was carried away with great care.

All of this caught us unawares. This strange and ugly rock had plummeted down from the heavens! It had once mended a hole in the sky, emitting light and warmth. Our ancestors perhaps stared up at it. It once filled them with brightness, hope and longing. Yet, it broke away and lay among the dirty earth and the wild grass for hundreds of years.

Grandma protested: "We didn't know it was so unusual. It was no good for building a wall or a step."

"Because it was too ugly?" The astronomer asked.

"Yeah, it's really too ugly."

"But this is where its beauty lies," the astronomer noted. "Its ugliness is the source of its beauty."

"Ugliness – the source of beauty?"

"Indeed. When ugliness becomes an all-surpassing quality, the end result is beauty. Simply because it was not an ordinary piece of hard rock, it could not be utilised as a wall or step. It couldn't be carved into a sculpture or used for beating laundry either. It wasn't destined for these menial tasks, so it was jeered at by worldly eyes."

Grandma's face became flushed in response, and so did mine.

I was filled with shame. Now I had come to know the greatness of the ugly stone. I had begrudged how it lay in repose for so many years and pathetically put up with all that befell it. I suddenly grasped, with a painful empathy, how it had weathered loneliness and never surrendered in the face of misunderstanding.

Two Generations

I.

Pa, you said that when you were young, you sought after love with a madness. But Pa, do you know, when you were circling around the blossom-heavy peach tree beneath the moonlight, when you were somersaulting in fields full of wildflowers, when a kind of boiling stream was coursing around your body, that was me, and I was searching for you too.

Pa, you said that when you married my mother, you were the happiest man in the world. But Pa, do you know, when you were tucking into the date that those teasing pals dangled over you on your wedding night, and on the first daybreak of your honeymoon as the everlasting candle on the windowsill burnt down into a knot, the core of that date was me and I was the wick of the lamp. From then on, you had a rival.

II.

Pa, you've always boasted that you are my mother's guardian. My kind mother offered her youth to you unselfishly. But Pa, do you know, after the conception, who was it that made my mother shy and as tender as a water lily, unable to bear the cold wind's chafe? And who was it that caused her to grow plump and full-figured like the mid-autumn moon? After the birth, who was responsible for her pink face losing its charming feminine sheen and glamour?

Pa, you've always been conceited and claimed you were my mother's keeper. And yet, it was my virtuous mother who lavished her concern upon you. And Pa, do you know, when I was in my mother's womb, were you brave enough to knead me gently? When my mother smiles to herself alone, is it for you? Can my mother tell you when it was you started to teethe? Can she say which of your teeth appeared first – was it from the upper or lower set? Did she hear the first wail of your life?

III.

Pa, you always worry about your white hair before the mirror. Do you know who stole the darkness? You often stroke your face and fret about your complexion. Do you know who spirited away its healthy blush? Pa, it was me, me. In front of my mother, we have been rivals. Sometimes I lost and you won, but in the end you lost outright. So, you envied me and were impatient towards me, beating me if you felt like it.

Pa, when your figure became more and more stooped, like a bowing willow tree, do you know who it was that put the kink in your waist? When your phlegm increased in volume and you wheezed incessantly, do you know who installed those rusty bellows in your throat? Pa, it was me, me. In front of my mother, we have been rivals. I lost and you won, but in the end you lost outright. So, you flattered me, let me scramble around your neck and called me "honey".

IV.

Oh, Pa, I know that there would be no me without you. But from the moment I emerged, I would become the one who would bury you. Even so, Pa, don't feel sad, don't feel envy and hatred. This you should try to understand: the child is its mother's proudest treasure. I belong to my mother. Didn't you once belong to yours? Oh Pa, I fully understand that when I appeared, my destiny was to bury you. Even so, Pa, don't feel sad, don't feel envy and hatred. You should remember: once you buried your own father, you did not forget that you were his son. Then, how can I ever forget you?

I am not a Good Son

Only after reaching the age of forty – and with that encountering many frustrations along my decades-long, hard-fought, high-flying career – did I realise my faults as a son. A mother is sacrosanct. She not only gives birth to her flesh and blood, but she does not expect her offspring to return the debt of life. Whether her child travels far away or stays close to home, she is the one who will provide succour to buoy his sense of kinship and strength, keeping him conscious of his roots. On life's journey as a man, his mother serves as the filling station.

My mother stayed in the countryside all her life. She was illiterate and tongue-tied with words. The closest she ever came to an aeroplane was witnessing its shadow in the clouds. She was not clear about my occupation in the distant city; she only knew that I could write. She told me once that when I scribbled away, my eyes blinked repeatedly. She would consequently become worried about the misery I might be enduring. She would ask: "Is it possible to finish writing all the words of the world?" Again and again, she tried to halt me in my tracks. Several years ago, when my mother came to reside in the city for a short while, she would pass her time sewing winter garments and other items for my child and me. Fearing that we might catch a chill, she would stuff extra cotton wadding into whatever she was making. As a result, when we wore her handiwork, the youngster and I resembled loping, ungainly bears. She was not accustomed to life in the city and complained that the food was too greasy and we had too many visitors and that the light in the sitting room was always on and that we threw everything away as soon as it became old. She lamented: "Life here isn't as orderly as it is in the country." The thing she found hardest to bear was that we beat and scolded our child. The infant did not cry, but she would. After we had patched matters up, she would be annoyed and return soon after to the countryside. Each time she visited us, she would arrive joyfully and then leave in a temper. After she had gone, I didn't miss her. Year in, year out, I did not even dream about her. My mother's compassion towards me was never appreciated. When success turned my head, her very existence slipped my mind. Yet, whenever I nursed a grievance or felt wronged, I wanted to tell her about it – grizzling in front of her.

My mother's surname was Zhou. I learnt this from my maternal uncle but he didn't divulge her given name. Once when I was twelve years old, I was trading curses with another child in the village – in the countryside the best way to vent one's gall is to yell out the names of your adversary's parents. That girl's father's name was Fish, so I blurted out: "Fish, fishy Fish lives in the river!" She jeered back: "Moth! Moth! Piffling Moth!" I knew then that my mother was "Little Moth Zhou".

A big shot is a big shot simply because his name is chanted by thousands. Up until then, I had not spoken my mother's name and I had seldom heard neighbours use this moniker. Yet, although she was no great luminary, her stature was not diminished by this omission. Her honesty, simplicity, goodness and industry were universally acknowledged in my hometown. Even now, there are some who deride me for retaining the bearing of a farmer. I don't feel any shame that I am the son of a farmer. My mother told me to have tolerance. So I have tolerated everything that I should and, consequently, have sidestepped many potential calamities. But my faults lie in the forbearance I have shown to the undeserving.

Seven years ago, my father had an operation for stomach cancer. My heart and thoughts were entirely with him. After he passed away, I still dreamed him up – still with his sickly pallor. When I woke up, I would weep, then buy some touchpaper to burn for him. Once the ashes from the paper had scattered, my thoughts would immediately switch to my mother. I would become restless for days until I sent her money. Then I was free to burrow myself into work with a clear conscience. In this state, her shadow never loomed in my heart. My neighbours in the village praised me for sending money. However, I came to understand that doing this had nothing to do with cherishing her. Rather, I was trying to rectify my own psychological imbalance. My mother could not bring herself to spend this gift. I heard my younger sister say that she couldn't find a place to store it, so she'd rolled the notes up and stuffed them into the cotton shoes under the bed. The rats nearly pilfered them as bedding. I complained to my mother, though her response was disappointing: "What's the use of me having so much cash? I'll just save up my spare change and pay you back in full when I can manage it. As long as you're all happy and in good health, I'm content to make do. But right now, I'm not in so pathetic a state that I have to drink un-boiled water."

Last year when I went back, she did indeed reimburse the money. I remember I then asked her to go to the country fair to buy nibbles. She brought back a great quantity of brown sugar which she tipped into a porcelain jar.

Whenever kids came to her place, she would dig three fingers into the jar and plug a pinch of sugar into their mouths. The children snook over the sweet stuff and went away sated. My mother would smile and scold: "Greedy puppies – you're all take, take, take and no give." Afterwards, she would stare blankly for a long time.

My mother's later years were lonely. We siblings discussed the issue and decided that she could care for my younger sister's children. Tiring as it might be, the time would pass more easily when she had the youngsters to care for. My little nephew duly became her tail, following her wherever she went. Once, grandma and grandson came together to the city. Her eyes grew moist when she saw the portrait of my deceased father hanging in the study. She said: "When a man is dead, it's easy to count the number of his days. I didn't realise that four years have passed." I tried to change the subject but the more I tried, the more tears trickled from her eyes. My little nephew came toward the photo impetuously and asked for "Grandpa". I thought this would increase her heartache, but she explained: "Your grandpa was buried under the earth." The child replied: "Anything that's put in the earth grows up again. How come my grandpa hasn't?" To my surprise, mother was not irritated; she broke into a wide smile.

My mother doted on the child and in public she would tease him for being without shame. He seemed to be physically growing, but every night he would search sleepily for a nipple. The child would flush with embarrassment and put his hands over my mother's mouth in fear. The grandmother and grandson would also wrestle on the ground and, being out of breath, she would smile. My younger sister and I criticised her for pampering him. She chided us: "I've never known an education myself – but it looks like you're all doing very well for yourselves." We could not outmanoeuvre her; deep down we hoped that the kid would remain as he was forever. Nonetheless, my nephew, like the crops, thrived once he had the blast of the wind upon him. Before we realised, it was time for him to enrol at school. My mother seemed quite lost. She continued to live in my younger sister's home. She was so anxious that the pent-up fire in her heart would break out and cause her lips to be chapped. I thought that if my mother was a believer in Buddhism, she could go to the temple every day to burn incense and chant *sutras* on her return home. My mother had no such faith. Later, the old grandmothers around her pulled her outdoors to practice *qigong* breathing exercises. We siblings felt a semblance of relief.

During my childhood, I had the impression that my mother looked after only the family's food and clothing. That was in the era of communal farming, so in the daytime she would go out to work with the Production Brigade, and in the evening, she was always rinsing radishes and slicing sweet potatoes or spinning thread and fashioning shoe soles. Otherwise, she would be weaving hemp, fastening the ends of the fibres onto the door latch. My mother didn't know how to prepare fancy fare though. Once a year, my father would be responsible for the single grand steaming bowl, though my mother was a skilled hand at kneading noodle dough. For this talent, she was renowned. If a visitor dropped by, my father would inevitably say: "Let's have noodles!" Then came the sound of the chopping board and the bellows. My mother would bring in several bowls of piping hot noodles, using the abacus as a tray. As the guests tucked in, the children would be sent out to play in the lanes. Before long, we would sneak back stealthily to look for leftovers. As expected, there was roughly a bowl-and-a-half swilling around the bottom of the cauldron. During those years of hardship, pure wheat flour noodles were only ever used to entertain guests. If no visitors came, we would satisfy ourselves by diluting the noodles with cracked corn porridge. My mother would season the porridge with pickles and diced vegetables, serving the mixture to my father and each of the children in turn. Last of all, her bowl would contain only the cracked corn and vegetables.

Over this period, food and wood were at a premium. Life was stark, but as children we were naturally buoyant. The most vexing thing was helping mother turn the grindstone. Usually she would begin to clean the stone after nightfall. She sifted together white corn and beans as a prelude to processing a composite flour. So huge was the grindstone that she could not rotate it unaided. She would ask my younger brother and I to take hold of the handle at the same time. The stars were scattered and the moon bright as we trod circuit after circuit around the axis. We persisted until our heads were dizzy and numb. When the first batch was ground, mother would sieve the grain. My younger brother and I dozed off, resting our heads against the stone. She would rouse us to restart the work, though we would insist: "That's enough, that's enough, Mother." Nevertheless, she explained the importance of repeatedly grinding until the bran was as thin as mosquito wings. We would quarrel and then her two sons would toss aside the handle in a fit of pique. My mother would sigh as she acquiesced, asking the neighbours for help. We would hear her plaintive calling, her begging, her imploring – all without reply.

"Sister-in-law, I'll repay you in kind; I'll help you with

the grindstone next time you do the job. The boys are off to school tomorrow; I daren't risk them missing class." My brother and I couldn't bear to see our mother laying herself at the mercy of others like this, so we rubbed our noses and reluctantly retrieved the handle.

She assiduously took care of all mundane domestic matters. But if major events arose, the last say was reserved for my father, who was a teacher and returned home only on Sundays. During the years when I was a university student, on the final evening of my vacation from study, we'd hold a family meeting. The main speaker was invariably my father. He would emphasise the importance of study, treating others with sincerity, the sayings of Confucius, and how humankind had always achieved success by hard graft alone. As he held forth for hours, mother would sit at his side rolling tapers for his water pipe. After she had twisted many into a pile, she was apt to nod off. At last, he would exclaim: "Does mother have her pennyworth?" She would jolt awake to further scolding. She could only smile and reply: "You're a teacher. What can I say? It's your unique talent to rabbit on." Everybody would laugh, point out that it was too late, and scatter for bed. Through all this my mother would be in high spirits. She would latch the courtyard gate and the pigsty, and check all the jars of perishables on the counter to see if the lids were secure against rodents. After everything was done, she would enter the kitchen alone and prepare boiled vegetable dumplings for my breakfast the next morning.

Following my father's passing, I intended to bring her to live with me in the city. She refused because the crucial third anniversary had not come around and she could not be sure his spirit was yet at rest. She was duty-bound to stay, offering up food at the altar every mealtime, in case my father's soul returned for a visit. When she had little to do and the weather was warm, she would trundle off to the village to play cards with the other grandmas. The standard stake was only one or two cents, so she carried with her twenty or thirty cents in loose notes stuffed down the back of her sock. Early in the morning, she would enter the chicken coop and poke a finger up every hen's bottom, testing for eggs. If they were on the brink of laying, she would break off her card game to collect the bounty. Perhaps surprisingly, she herself rarely ate eggs. With visitors, she would pretend to boil water for tea, but instead push a pot of poached eggs on her guests.

Every year, when plums ripened in the courtyard, she would always ask people to take some for me in the city. Should no one be willing to act as courier, the fruit would be stored until my return. "Ping is fond of sour fruit." Those words would hover on her lips. She wouldn't tip the fruits away until they were rotted to mush.

She trained herself in the practices of *qigong* at my younger sister's home, so that when I dropped in to see her, she dragged me over to the side room with great urgency. She commanded me to drink some cool water from a bottle she was waving around enthusiastically. After some probing, she explained that the bottled substance was "information water" from a *qigong* master and could cure the whole gamut of world illnesses. She said: "You should drink. Afterwards, your liver ailment will be cleared up completely." I consumed half. She brought me apples and oranges, introducing these similarly as "information fruits".

My mother never cared if I became a big shot or specialist. But neither did she know the honour of my occupation.

I never shared with her the tribulations and gloom encountered in my work. When *The Abandoned Capital* whipped up press both at home and abroad, she never passed a single comment on critics' praise or whatever attack had been recently meted out to me. But when she heard that I was ill and alone in hospital, through tears she asked my brothers and sisters to escort her to visit me. They forbade the trip, unwilling to part with their time. She poked an accusing finger at each of them, enraged. Later, she arrived anyway amidst a storm. Something was certainly amiss with her eyes. Duly, she wept and said: "What kind of a fate is this for my child?"

I reassured my mother that my lot was far from poor. Every kind of suffering I had experienced was tolerable. In my adolescent years, I would carry fifty kilos of firewood on my shoulders and walk along the narrow paths at the mountain's edge. Resting places were scarce, so no matter how painful one's shoulder and legs were, you had to go on. I cultivated a sort of power of forbearance.

The bitterest issue was that I was unable to wait on my mother in person. With my father gone, I should have, as the eldest son, assumed the responsibility for ensuring her happy dotage. Nonetheless, I found myself unable to care for her now and she was also consumed with worry about me. What kind of a son was I? Accompanying my mother out of the hospital, I took out all the money I had, saying: "Money cannot be any substitute for filial piety. But this is all I can do right now." She understood me and accepted the wad, gripping it tightly in her palm. She then shook my collar until it was arranged in good order and touched my face, observing that my beard was too long. A hot towel should be applied as a compress and then the whiskers neatly shorn away. I watched her bus crawling gradually away until I lost sight of it. I returned to my ward, lay on my bed, and reinserted the drip. Then the tears rolled.

Drafted on the hospital ward, 27th November 1993

Written for My Mother

When the people around us are alive, we are not so mindful about day turning into night turning into day. Once a person has passed away, the days pile up. According to my reckoning, in twenty days' time it will be the third anniversary of my mother's death.

During the last three years, I have been seized by a queer sensation. Namely, I have felt that my mother is not actually gone. I have also felt that my mother shares this sense that she has not departed. It is said that dying is like going to sleep, but while the sleeper knows he lies on a bed, he does not know exactly when he's drifted off.

For fourteen years, my mother lived with me in Xi'an. After a serious bout of illness, the doctor declared each of her organs was in a state of terminal exhaustion. So, I decided to send her back to Dihua, where she could continue to receive medical care. Every day in the village, she knew that her children would supply the drip with a constant feed of intravenous medicine. She closed her eyes and rested. On the third night, with her closed, she asked my younger sister to rinse her facecloth. But she must have been fading, for she never regained consciousness. Her comb lay beside the pillow. The key tied to her belt remained unused. She did not convey any final wishes.

Years ago, whenever I sneezed, I would always ask, "Who is missing me?". My mother loved to crack jokes. She would pick up where I left off and say, "Who is missing you? Your mother is missing you!". In the years since her death, I have sneezed with greater regularity. Usually, when I am late for a meal or stay up for too long, I sneeze. When I sneeze, I am certain my mother is still missing me.

My mother is missing me. She does not believe that she has passed away. I am ever more convinced that she is still alive. This feeling is especially intense when I stay quietly alone at home. Often, when I am writing I will suddenly hear my mother calling me. The voice is real and sincere. On hearing her call, I twist my head to the right; my mother used to perch on the edge of the bed in the room to the right-hand side of my study. When I craned over to begin my writing, she would stop walking and keep silent. Her eyes would remain fixed on me. After staring at me for a substantial amount of time, she would call my name and ask: "Is it possible to finish writing all the words of the world? Go out, take a walk." Now, when I think I hear my mother calling, I lay down my pen and head towards the voice. Has my mother travelled to Xi'an from Dihua? I stand for a long time. I repeat to myself that my mother has returned, she's just popped out to buy my favourite green peppers and radishes. Perhaps she is pulling my leg, hiding behind her portrait on the wall. I burn incense in front of the picture and mouth: "I am not tired."

Since her death, I have composed dozens of articles for others, but not a single character for my mother. In the eyes of all children, their mothers are great and kind, and I do not want to repeat the cliché. My mother was an ordinary woman with bound feet. She was illiterate and she held a peasant's household registration certificate. My mother was my mother, and of huge importance. After the longest time, the thought of her illness no longer brings my heart into my mouth. And yet whenever I prepare to venture to a distant place, there is no longer anybody to nag me to do this and that. When I am gifted fine food and drink, I no longer know to whom I should send them.

In my home in Xi'an, I haven't touched the furniture in my mother's room. Everything is as it was. Except I haven't glimpsed my mother's shadow. Again and again, I have repeated gravely to myself: "My mother is not dead. She has gone to live in the countryside." This summer it is too hot and humid. Every night when the heat and humidity wake me, I remind myself to install a new air-conditioner for my mother. With a jolt, I come back to my senses, comforting myself with the thought of her new place in the countryside. I imagine a house, breezy and cool.

The third anniversary draws closer. As per the custom, we will hold a special ceremony. I am preparing candles, incense and fruit, ready to go back to Dihua. But once I return to Dihua, I must visit her grave. The reality is that I am on the ground and she is beneath it. Life and death separate us forever now. I hear myself wailing amidst the tears.

Acknowledgements

The author and translators wish to thank Jamie McGarry and Valley Press for bringing this book to fruition. Thanks are also due to Dr. J. Graham Jones and Madeleine Hamey-Thomas for their assistance in proofreading.

Sponsorship was provided by First-class Universities and Academic Programs at Northwest University.